Radical GRACE

Radical GRACE

Justice for the Poor and Marginalized

Charles Wesley's Views for the Twenty-First Century

S T KIMBROUGH, JR.

WITH A FOREWORD BY **STANLEY HAUERWAS**

CASCADE *Books* · Eugene, Oregon

RADICAL GRACE
Justice for the Poor and Marginalized—Charles Wesley's Views for the Twenty-First
Century

Cascade Books
An Imprint of Wipf and Stock Publishers
199 W. 8th Ave., Suite 3
Eugene, OR 97401

www.wipfandstock.com

ISBN 13: 978-1-62032-143-0

Cataloging-in-Publication data:

Kimbrough, S. T., 1936–

Radical grace : justice for the poor and marginalized—Charles Wesley's views for the twenty-first century / S T Kimbrough, Jr. ; foreword by Stanley Hauerwas.

xvi + 134 p.; 23 cm—Includes bibliographical references and index(es).

ISBN 978-1-62032-143-0

1. Wesley, Charles, 1707–1788. 2. Church work with the poor—Methodist Church—History. 3. Hymns, English—History and criticism. 4. I. Hauerwas, Stanley, 1940–. II. Title.

BX8495.W4 K566 2013

Manufactured in the USA.

Unless otherwise noted, the translations of the Psalms in chapter 6 are from *Psalms for Praise and Worship*, ed. John Holbert, S T Kimbrough Jr., and Carlton R. Young. Nashville: Abingdon, 1992. *Psalms for Praise and Worship* (cited as NRSV/PPW below) contains adapted and edited quotations from the *New Revised Standard Version of the Bible*, used by permission.

The following congregational musical settings of Charles Wesley hymn texts are copyrighted © 2001 The Charles Wesley Society, Archives and History Center, Drew University, 36 Madison Ave., Madison, NJ, 07940: "The golden rule she has pursued," "The poor as Jesus' bosom friends," "Which of the Christians now," "Would you require what cannot be," "Help us to help each other," "You pastors hired who undertake," "Your duty let the Apostle show," and "Happy the multitude." All rights reserved. Used by permission.

The following congregational musical setting of the Charles Wesley hymn text "Your duty let the Apostle show" by Timothy E. Kimbrough is copyrighted © 1993 General Board of Global Ministries, GBGMusik, 475 Riverside Drive, New York, NY, 10115. All rights reserved. Used by permission.

Contents

Foreword: Poetry and the Poor

Lessons Learned from Charles Wesley and S T Kimbrough, Jr.

Methodism, in the beginning a movement among "the not well off," became the exemplification of bourgeois Christianity. Methodism is the faith of the middle class. That characterization may fail to do justice to British Methodism. In England, where the class structure is well determined and acknowledged, Methodist discipline helped many rise from poverty to become well established, but their class origins continued to determine how they understood themselves. As a result Methodism in England became identified with the Labor Party on its knees. At least that was the case when the Labor Party *was* the party of people like Tony Benn.

The middle-class character of Methodism in America did not result in a politics exemplified by the Labor Party. Methodism in America, at least Methodism at the beginning of the turn of the last century, was identified with a people who took pride in having worked hard to become respectable. They did not necessarily think of themselves as middle class. Rather they thought they were neither very rich nor very poor. They simply had "just enough." The "enough" that they had, however, they were pretty sure they deserved. They were generous people willing to share some of their "enough" with those who did not have "enough." But they did worry about giving what they had to those who seemed to have no desire to escape being poor.

I am, of course, characterizing what has become known as mainstream Methodism. Methodism produced break-off movements such as the Free Methodists, the Nazarenes, and the Salvation Army. These movements were constituted by working-class people, whose jobs or finances would not be sufficient for them to be understood as middle class. Accordingly, they found themselves still identified with the working poor.

My description of mainstream Methodism in America may seem not to take account of the involvement of Methodists as individuals and as a church in the Social Gospel movement. It is certainly the case that Methodists were among the early leaders in organizations created by advocates of the Social Gospel. But the Social Gospel was primarily a movement of the middle class. Thus, advocates of the Social Gospel, in the name of dealing with structural poverty, sought to develop social policies that could be enacted by government to end poverty. The significance of such a strategy is not to be discounted, but it is nonetheless a strategy of a bourgeois church and social order. The Christian duty is now thought to be getting governments to do what Christians no longer were sure the church or individual Christians were willing to do.

I begin with these observations about Methodism because I hope they will help us appreciate the significance of S T Kimbrough's account of Charles Wesley's commitment to the poor. Of course, Kimbrough has said what needs to be said in his concluding remarks about the implications of Charles Wesley's model for the church's obligation to the poor for the twenty-first century. I have little to add to his highlighting the importance of enduring concern, the importance of acquiring the virtues, the living out of divine grace, as well as the importance of memory for understanding why and how the poor must be the center of the life of the church. My task, however, is to suggest why Kimbrough's suggestions about the implications of Charles Wesley's understanding of the duty of Christians to preach the Gospel to the poor entails a theological position that was largely lost when Methodists became a church of the middle class.

The imagination of a middle-class church concerning the poor is restrained by the presumption that the task of the church is to make the poor well-off enough to be middle class. Therefore the church and Christians think of the poor primarily as people who need to have something done to or for them. In the process, "the poor" become an abstraction. We do not need to know those we identify as poor, we do not need to listen to the poor, we, that is the church, just need to do something for the poor. We simply cannot imagine that we might need to be with the poor. But because we cannot imagine what it might mean to be with the poor, we cannot imagine what it might mean to be with Christ.

What Kimbrough helps us see is this: Charles Wesley saw quite clearly that how the poor are understood is a christological issue. For Charles

Wesley, the poor could not be turned into an abstraction because Christ cannot be turned into an abstraction. That is why his poetry celebrating the lives of particular people who refused to abandon the poor is so important. They witness to the One that was at once poor and who cared for the poor.

We do well to pay particular attention to Charles Wesley's poem:

> Savior, how few there are
> Who thy condition share,
> Few, who cordially embrace,
> Love, and prize thy poverty,
> Want on earth a resting place,
> Needy and resigned like thee!

What strikes one when reading Kimbrough's account of Charles Wesley's understanding of our duty to the poor is that the poor for him were actual people; they were to be cared for, but equally important was the ability to be a friend to them. It is, after all, love that draws the poor to us just as it is love that draws the poor to the church. So the poor are not simply people Christians need so that we might do some "good," but the poor are God's people who make it possible to celebrate with the Father the Son's obedience even in the face of death.

Perhaps nothing makes Kimbrough's account of Charles Wesley's understanding of the Eucharist more compelling than his suggestion that the poor have spiritual as well as material needs. It is not simply the well-off who must be ready to sell their possessions, but the poor also can be possessed by what they do not possess. So it is surely right that Charles Wesley understood his preaching to the poor and their sharing in the meal of communion with Christ to be constitutive of what justice looks like when it is shaped by the love that is God's very life. Kimbrough rightly describes this participation as *theosis,* that is, the very participation of our lives in God's life. *Theosis* is often thought to be some ideal not reachable, but in Charles Wesley's understanding of what it means to be poor and to be with the poor, we begin to understand that this is no unrealizable ideal but the very substance of the life of the church. *Theosis* turns out to be the expression of Matthew 25. So understood, we gain a glimpse of what it means for all humankind to be made one through the love of God.

Accordingly, Charles Wesley's christological understanding of what it means for the church not only to care for the poor but also to be the church of the poor makes clear that his christological understanding of the poor is inseparable from his understanding of the church. In particular, it is the worship of God that is the heart of what it means for the church to be the church of the poor. For it is in worship that any distinction between the poor and those who are not poor is called into question and even obliterated.

It may seem odd to think that the church's first responsibility to the poor is to provide right worship of God, but it turns out that the poor know better than others what they need. Through worship, through the beauty of liturgy, they discover, in a manner that those who are not poor do not, that there is no standing more significant for learning our worth than learning to kneel before God. That Kimbrough ends his reflections on Charles Wesley's accounts of his preaching to and care of the poor with "worship resources" is a gift to the poor.

I think it is, moreover, no accident that the one who rediscovered the christological significance of the poor was a poet. The worship of God depends on the language honed from souls shaped by the love of God—a love recognized most intensely by those not satiated by the goods of the world. Charles Wesley was an extraordinary poet whose poetry enabled us to sing that the poor and the not-so-poor could be united in one voice. As odd as it might seem, that unity turns out to be not only what is needed if the church called Methodist is to be renewed, but the unity thereby discovered is the hope of the church as a whole, and of the world.

STANLEY HAUERWAS
Gilbert T. Rowe Professor of Theological Ethics
The Divinity School
Duke University
Durham, NC

Acknowledgments

The author expresses gratitude to Dr. Carlton R. Young for a variety of suggestions for this volume, to Dr. Stanley Hauerwas for his careful reading of the text and his encouraging emphasis on the importance of the volume for the church of the twenty-first century, and to The Divinity School of Duke University for making its valuable research resources available.

Abbreviations

JOHN AND CHARLES WESLEY

HSP (1739) — *Hymns and Sacred Poems*, 1739

HSP (1740) — *Hymns and Sacred Poems*, 1740

HSP (1742) — *Hymns and Sacred Poems*, 1742

Poet. Works — George Osborn, editor. *The Poetical Works of John and Charles Wesley*. 13 vols., 1868–72

Whitsunday Hymns — *Hymns of Petition and Thanksgiving for the Promise of the Father*, 1746

CHARLES WESLEY

Jackson, *Journal* — Thomas Jackson, editor. *The Journal of the Rev. Charles Wesley, M.A.* 2 vols., 1849

HSP (1749) — *Hymns and Sacred Poems*. 2 vols., 1749

Hymns of Intercession — *Hymns of Intercession for All Mankind*, 1758

MSJ — S T Kimbrough, Jr., and Kenneth G. C. Newport, editors. *The Manuscript Journal of the Reverend Charles Wesley, M.A.* 2 vols., 2007

Redemption Hymns (1747) — *Hymns for those that seek and those that have Redemption in the Blood of Jesus Christ*, 1747

Resurrection Hymns (1746) — *Hymns for our Lord's Resurrection*, 1746

Rep. Verse — Frank Baker, editor. *Representative Verse of Charles Wesley*, 1962

Scripture Hymns

(1762)   *Short Hymns on Select Passages of the Holy Scriptures.* 2
               vols., 1762

Unpub. Poetry   S T Kimbrough, Jr., and Oliver A. Beckerlegge, edi-
               tors. *The Unpublished Poetry of Charles Wesley.* 3 vols.,
               1988–1992

OTHER ABBREVIATIONS

AV/KJV   King James Version of the Bible (1611); Authorized Version of
               the Church of England

BCP   Book of Common Prayer

UMH   *The United Methodist Hymnal* (1989)

Introduction

The situation of the poor and marginalized of eighteenth-century British society was desperate. It is estimated that roughly half of the population were considered poor when measured by the government standards of the time. Poverty was rampant. There was extensive unemployment, vast economic displacement, and physical and mental infirmities due to lack of medical care, poor sanitation, and malnutrition.

In the view of many politicians and economists, the poor were thought to be a detriment to society. The Poor Relief Act of 1601 was supposed to establish a system of relief for the poor. It sought to develop programs to aid the weak and infirm, to employ those who were able, and to provide assistance to those in need. In these ways one hoped to bolster the nation's economy. In a sense the Poor Relief Act humanized some aspects of dealing with the poor, as earlier laws had allowed for beggars and vagrants to be branded and enslaved for at least two years. Beggars could be whipped, or even executed if they were caught in a third offense. "The Poor Laws were designed to take care of the infirm and to furnish work for the underemployed, not to provide maintenance for the unemployed. The original theory and design may have been admirable to some, but in practice it failed miserably."[1]

The Workhouse Act of 1723 mandated local parishes to erect workhouses for the poor. Even so, the requirement was generally not followed due to the high costs involved for such a building. Some parishes sought less expensive ways to assist the poor.

Workhouses tended to become havens for the sick, senile, and infirm. Orphanages were to be places of security for destitute and often abandoned children, who were to become apprentices in various jobs. Nevertheless, both often became hovels of illiteracy, thievery, corruption, sickness, and abuse. As there were no child labor laws, children were often exploited and abused in despicable ways in the labor market

1. Heitzenrater, *Poor and the People Called Methodists*, 213. See Woloch, *Eighteenth-Century Europe*.

of eighteenth-century England. Many aspects of the exploitation of children have been chronicled in some of the plates of the eighteenth-century graphic artist William Hogarth.

The treatment of the poor and the Poor Laws were not without their critics,[2] both negative and positive, and while there were some efforts to improve the living and working conditions of the poor, on the whole these efforts failed.

Those controlling the economy did not really want the poor to move upward out of their poverty. Joseph Townsend[3] in large measure saw the Poor Laws as providing guaranteed welfare for the indigent and those who had no desire to work and deemed it healthy and essential for the English economy to maintain the servant/master relationship.

It should not be assumed, however, that there were no philanthropic endeavors to aid the poor and destitute. There were, but they were often the efforts of individuals (or groups of individuals) such as Captain Thomas Coram, who, with the aid of public subscriptions, enabled the establishment in 1742 of the Foundling Hospital, which became a place of refuge for unwanted and abandoned infants and children. One should mention as well the Greenwich Hospital, which was opened in 1705 to receive wounded sailors of the Royal Navy and Mercantile Marine and was praised for its cleanliness, watchful care, and provisions for the patients.

The legal and penal system of the eighteenth century readily enabled the exploitation of the poor. There was no organized police force, and constables, if they could be found, were often unpaid. Once convicted of a crime, one could be hanged, transported to the New World and there sold into servitude, or possibly pardoned. One's indentured servitude might be limited according to the nature of the offense. After 1776, those not held in jails and doomed to transportation might have been confined to an old ship stripped of its fittings and moored on the Thames or even shipped out to Australia. The transportation scheme was fraught with difficulties and essentially failed at first because the government refused to fund it. After

---

2. See M'Farlan, *Inquiries Concerning the Poor*; Townsend, *Dissertation on the Poor Laws*; Holroyd, Earl of Sheffield, *Observations on the Impolicy, Abuses, and False Interpretations of the Poor Laws*; Bailey, *Treatise on the Better Employment, and more Comfortable Support, of the Poor in Workhouses*. See also Appendix 3 in Heitzenrater's *Poor and the People Called Methodists* for an annotated description of each of the above volumes.

3. *Dissertation on the Poor Laws*.

1718 the government agreed to pay £3 per convict, which seemed to give the system a brief reprieve.

Defense of the poor in a legal system that favored the elite and successful was practically impossible without a connection to someone in a position of authority.[4]

Much has been written about John and Charles Wesley's life and ministry with the poor. It is common knowledge that they spent much of their ministry among the marginalized peoples of Great Britain—in the workhouses of major cities and with the colliers of the hearths of Newcastle and elsewhere. John Wesley expressed his concern for medical care for the poor by opening a clinic at the Foundery[5] in London, which he purchased in 1739, and his little book *Primitive Physic* was written to provide medical advice at no cost to the owner of the book. Both brothers preached to the less fortunate throughout England, Scotland, Wales, and Ireland. They started schools for children who had no educational opportunities and established orphanages to care for destitute and abandoned children.

All of these activities are well known, but what was it within the depth of their faith and ethical commitment that inspired them to such action? In the last two decades much has been written about this subject, particularly from the perspectives of John Wesley.[6] In this study, however, the focus is primarily on Charles Wesley.

While the two brothers are often linked in their thought and faith posture, Charles grew up more under the influence of his eldest brother Samuel, than John. Charles attended Westminster School where Samuel was an usher, and John attended Charterhouse School. Samuel too became an Anglican priest with a high regard for the Church of England, its Articles of Religion, and its liturgies. He was also a gifted poet, and Charles records that after Samuel became the head of Tiverton School, he would often visit in his home and make copies of his poems. It is interesting that

---

4. See Beattie, *Crime and the Courts in England, 1660–1800,* and King, *Crime, Justice, and Discretion in England, 1740–1820.*

5. For background on the Foundery and its multifaceted use by Wesley, see Kimbrough and Young, *John Wesley's First Tune Book,* ix–xiv.

6. Marquardt, *Praxis und Prinzipien der Sozialethik John Wesleys [John Wesley's Social Ethics]*; Jennings, *Good News to the Poor*; Meeks, *Portion of the Poor*; Heitzenrater, *Poor and the People Called Methodists*; Walsh, "John Wesley and the Community of Goods"; Tamez, "Wesley as Read by the Poor"; Miles, "Works of Mercy as Spiritual Formation." See also Hughes, "Wesleyan Roots of Christian Socialism"; Rieger, *Remember the Poor*; Warner, *Wesleyan Movement in the Industrial Revolution*; Meeks, *God the Economist.*

the idea of a medical dispensary for the poor in the Westminster section of London was first suggested by Samuel, and this may have had a strong influence on his brothers John and Charles.

The primary sources for this study are Charles's comments in his sermons and *Manuscript Journal* regarding life and ministry with the poor, and those of his poems that articulate the ethical responsibility and the theological *raison d'être* for reaching out to and caring for the poor. We begin with the sermons.

I. The Sermons

While I have maintained elsewhere[1] that Charles Wesley was a lyrical theologian as reflected in his poetry, clearly Kenneth G. C. Newport has made anew the case, based on Charles's sermon corpus, that he was a theologian in his own right who, as a biblical interpreter, employed exegetical methods of his own day and was a serious theological interpreter of Scripture and the Christian faith. "In places," says Newport, "his exegesis is highly unusual, perhaps even novel, and his reasoning tight and mature."[2] Ted Campbell speaks of Charles Wesley as a *theologos* "in the sense in which the term is used in Eastern Christian churches which speak of the author of the Fourth Gospel as 'St John *Theologos*. . . . [i.e.] one who gives us words (*logoi*) about God (*theos*).'"[3] Both Newport's and Campbell's perspectives are a helpful corrective to the view that Charles was only and primarily an "experiential theologian."[4] As important as experience was for him, he was able to complement it with conjecture and reason. "It is in prose not poetry that Charles is more clearly seen to apply the logician's art."[5] Therefore, it is important to recognize, as have Newport, J. Ernest Rattenbury,[6] Luke Wiseman,[7] Franz Hillenbrandt,[8] and John Tyson,[9] that Charles stands on his own as a theologian. Furthermore, he did not simply reproduce his brother John's views in his prose and poetry, as close as they stood on many theological issues.

1. See Kimbrough, *Lyrical Theology of Charles Wesley.*

2. Newport, *Sermons of Charles Wesley.*

3. "Charles Wesley *Theologos*," 264–65.

4. See Rattenbury, *Evangelical Doctrines of Charles Wesley's Hymns,* 85–107.

5. Newport, *Sermons of Charles Wesley,* 52.

6. Ibid.

7. *Charles Wesley, Evangelist and Poet,* 111–54.

8. Hildebrandt and Beckerlegge, *Collection of Hymns for the Use of the People Called Methodists,* 7:1–22.

9. *Charles Wesley on Sanctification.*

Unquestionably foundational to his view of justice for the poor and marginalized is Charles's theology of salvation, which one finds elaborated in his sermons and hymns. It is thus important to emphasize that his poetry is not the only source of his theology. He stands staunchly within an Arminian/Wesleyan interpretation of salvation. His poetry is filled with the celebration of God's free gift of salvation that is available to everyone.

> Outcasts of men, to you I call,[10]
>   Harlots and publicans and thieves!
> He spreads his arms to embrace you all,
>   Sinners alone his grace receives:
> No need of him the righteous have,
> He came the lost to seek and save.
>
> Harlots, and publicans and thieves,[11]
>   In holy triumph join!
> Saved is the sinner that believes
>   From crimes as great as mine!
> Murtherers and all ye hellish crew,
>   Ye sons of lust and pride,
> Believe the Saviour died for you;
>   For me the Saviour died.

All of humankind is helpless without God's intervention in Jesus Christ, through whom all may be redeemed. It is this intervention that imbues each individual with the love of God and others, the only viable motivation for human behavior. Indeed, through this love one participates in God's nature, and love enables a life of piety and a life of good works.

Susan White rightly avers that "love . . . is the beginning and end of Charles Wesley's theological vision, with all other characteristics of mind, heart and action radiating from that centre in concentric circles. . . . Charles' presumption is that since love is the essence of God and of the God-human relationship, the understanding of which is the object of our theological quest, it is only by approaching the task with love that we can

---

10. Charles's hymn "Christ, the Friend of Sinners," in *HSP* (1939), 102.

11. Stanzas 15 and 16 from the eighteen-stanza hymn, "For the Anniversary Day of One's Conversion," from which the hymn "O for a thousand tongues to sing" comes. *HSP* (1740), 122.

hope to know when we have come close to the truth."[12] The expanse and extent of this love is immeasurable. It is

> Love immense and unconfined,[13]
> Love to all of humankind.

Though Charles does have his moments of darkness, he is confident that God will indeed redeem all sinners and that the redemptive love that fills them will strengthen the community of the faithful not only in worship and devotion, but also in acts of compassion and goodwill.

In two of his sermons that postdate his conversion of May 21, 1738, one discovers the theological foundation for his perspectives on reaching out to the poor and marginalized, which he greatly expands in his poetry.

THE SERMON BASED ON TITUS 3:8

> This is a faithful saying, and these things I will that thou affirm constantly, that they which have believed in God might be careful to maintain good works.[14]

Charles addresses a very controversial matter in eighteenth-century theological discussions, namely, the relationship of faith and works. In the Wesleyan-Arminian tradition, it was clear that good works were absolutely essential. They could not be averted by an overemphasis on faith. Charles emphasizes that faith indeed is the one true way through which Christ is formed in one's life, but to aver that faith without works is sufficient is in an inadequate response to the grace of God.

In this sermon Charles writes:

> If Christ be given for us, he is likewise given to us; he is formed in our hearts by faith, and lives and reigns in our souls. . . . They are good that do good, being conformed both outwardly and inwardly to Christ Jesus; in whom neither circumcision availeth anything, nor uncircumcision, but a new creature.[15]

. . .

12. "Charles Wesley and Contemporary Theology," 523.

13. *HSP* (1749), 1:38, lines 113–14 of a 162–line poem titled "The Beatitudes."

14. The sermon on this text was preached by Charles on Dec. 21, 1738; Jan. 14, 1739; Mar. 4, 1739.

15. Newport, *Sermons of Charles Wesley,* 164–65.

God rewardeth every man according to his works, that the more our works, the more will be our reward. May you therefore improve every talent to the utmost; having obtained mercy, may you labour more abundantly. Let it be your meat to do the will of your Father. Let it be your constant employment to serve and relieve your Saviour in his poor distressed members.

He gives you now a blessed opportunity. For inasmuch as you do it to one of the least of these his children, you do it unto him. He himself has assured you that whosoever shall give a cup of cold water to one of these little ones in the name of a disciple, he shall in no wise lose its [sic] reward. Above all give charity because this is the noblest, as taking in both body and soul. What you give them is given toward training up so many candidates for eternity, and the love of little children is now waiting to receive it at your hands.

Indeed whenever you do an alms, you should do it unto the Lord and not unto man. You should see and revere your Saviour in every poor man you ease, and be as ready to relieve him as you would to relieve Christ himself.

Is Christ, is he, an hungered? Give him meat. Is he thirsty? Give him drink. Is he a stranger? Take ye him in. Clothe him when he is naked; visit him when he is sick. When he is in prison, come ye unto him. So shall he say unto you when he comes in his glory, and all the holy angels with him, 'Come ye blessed of my Father, inherit the kingdom prepared for you from the foundation of the world.'[16]

This sermon excerpt embodies the fundamental theological perspective of Charles Wesley that guides his behavior: "Let it be your constant employment to serve and relieve your Saviour in his poor distressed members." "Constant employment" implies all of one's human activity. In such engagement one is serving Christ the Savior, for there is no division between service to Christ and service to others. To serve one is to serve the other.

Years later, Charles articulated this eloquently in a stanza from a lengthy poem remembering the faithful life of Mary Naylor.

Her Saviour in his members seen,[17]
A stranger she received him in,
    An hungry Jesus fed,
Tended her sick, imprisoned Lord,

16. Ibid., 164–66.
17. *Funeral Hymns* (1759), 53.

And flew in all his wants to afford
  Her ministerial aid.

This one stanza about Mary Naylor is an eloquent lyrical summary of what Charles said in the sermon on Titus 3:8: "Is Christ, is he, an hungered? Give him meat. Is he thirsty? Give him drink. Is he a stranger? Take ye him in. Clothe him when he is naked; visit him when he is sick. When he is in prison, come ye unto him."

This twofold service to Christ and others Wesley sees as a "blessed opportunity." He then draws on two passages from the Gospel of Matthew to describe the nature of such opportunity: "For inasmuch as you do it to one of the least of these his children, you do it unto him" (25:40);[18] and "whosoever shall give a cup of cold water to one of these little ones in the name of a disciple, he shall in no wise lose its [sic] reward."[19] A holistic and integrated view of *diakonia* is at the heart of Charles Wesley's theology and is central to his outreach to the poor and marginalized. Not only are Christ and those one serves seen as one, but he views charity as the noblest human gesture, for it integrates the body and soul of the Christian. Thus, it engages the whole person.

Charles says something very interesting about almsgiving, namely, there is a sense of priority that should dominate one's charity. One should not think of doing something for someone else *per se*; rather, all acts of charity should be done as unto God. He states it this way:

> Indeed whenever you do an alms, you should do it unto the Lord and not unto man. You should see and revere your Saviour in every poor man you ease, and be as ready to relieve him as you would to relieve Christ himself.

Many years after composing and preaching this sermon, Wesley wrote:

> Members of his Church we know
>   The poor his body are:
> All the goods he had below,
>   They should his garments share:

18. AV: Inasmuch as ye have done it unto one of the least of these my brethren, ye have done it unto me.

19. AV: And whosoever shall give to drink unto one of these little ones a cup of cold water only in the name of a disciple, verily I say unto you, he shall in no wise lose his reward.

> But the greedy soldiers seize
> What should supply his people's need,
> Leave the members in distress
> And neither clothe nor feed.[20]

The poor are seen as members of Christ's body, the church. This is a perspective often ignored in discussions of ecclesiology, but for Wesley, such an understanding is fundamental to the nature of the church and to Christian ethical posture. It is at the heart of radical grace, for it claims for the church what the church often does not claim for itself. Historically, the church has set its own boundaries and requirements for membership, which often have excluded the poor.

THE SERMON BASED ON JOHN 4:41

> But whosoever drinketh of the water that I shall give him shall never thirst; but the water that I shall give him shall be in him a well of water, springing up into everlasting life.

Wesley preached this sermon based on a text from John's Gospel in 1739, 1740, and 1742. It includes two important passages for this discussion:

> if [the Christian] employ himself in any external acts of moral or instituted duty, he does it freely, not of necessity. In acts of charity, he gives from a principle of love to God, and man for God's sake, and so cheerfully, not grudgingly. His alms are not wrung out of him, but proceed from him, as a stream from its fountain.[21]

In this first quotation, Wesley emphasizes the importance of free will in all "acts of moral or instituted duty." No one is forced to act beneficently toward others. One is not required to aid others. Wesley says the determining factor is "a principle of love to God, and man for God's sake." This "principle of love" is central to Charles Wesley's theology and all human action. If we do what we do for others merely out of a sense of duty, our actions may be well meaning but fraught with wrong intention. Furthermore, one does acts of charity with a joyous spirit, or "cheerfully," and by no means "grudgingly." Such acts are done out of free volition; they are not "wrung out" of someone. Wesley uses a wonderful metaphor to describe

---

20. *Unpub. Poetry*, 2:67; stanza one of a hitherto unpublished poem based on Mark 15:24, "When they had crucified him, they parted his garments . . ."

21. Newport, *Sermons of Charles Wesley*, 262.

how acts of charity should proceed from everyone: "they proceed [from us], as a stream from its fountain." Just as water freely emerges from a fountain, so good deeds toward others flow unendingly from Christ's followers, who are filled, first and foremost, with a sense of love for God, all humankind, and all creation.

This "principle of love to God and man for God's sake" is for Wesley the key to all human behavior. God is the author of this principle, and through it God has made all humankind partakers of the divine nature.

> The author of this free principle is God himself, the free agent, the fountain of his own acts, who hath made it a partaker of his own nature. The uncreated life and liberty hath given this privilege to the religious soul, in some sense to have life and liberty in itself. In nothing does the soul more resemble the divine essence than in this noble freedom, which may therefore justly claim the free spirit for its author, (Ps 51:12; 2 Cor 3:17) or the Son of God for its original [*sic*], according wto that of S. Joh (8:36 'If the Son shall make you free, then shall you be free indeed').[22]

It is interesting that Charles connects the function of this "principle of love of God and man" with the concept of *theosis*. He avers that God "hath made it a partaker of his own nature." Through the fulfillment of the "principle of love," one becomes a partaker in God's own nature. In other words, there is an integration of faith and works inspired by love through which participation in God's nature is enabled. This is a fulcrum of Wesley's theology of outreach to the poor and marginalized. We are totally free to act on behalf of others, and we do so emboldened and enabled by the "principle of love."

---

22. Ibid., 263.

II. The Manuscript Journal

A month after his conversion on May 21, 1738, Charles recorded in the *MSJ*[1] a theological perspective that is formative for his attitude toward the poor and shapes his action on their behalf.

> **Thursday, June 22 [1738].** Comforted Hetty[2] under a strong temptation, because she was not in all points affected like other believers, especially the poor, who have generally a much larger degree of confidence than the rich and learned. I had a proof of this today after Mrs Searl's, where meeting a poor woman, and convincing her of unbelief, I used a prayer for her that God who hath chosen the poor of this world to be rich in faith, would now impart to her his unspeakable gift. In the midst of the prayer she received it; avowed it openly and increased visibly therein.[3]

Though it could not have been a popular position in eighteenth-century England, Charles believed most sincerely that "the poor . . . have generally a much larger degree of confidence than the rich and learned." This view is central to a theology of radical grace. The society was controlled in large measure by the landed gentry, to whom the Church of England had innumerable ties. Given the wealth and the extensive land and property holdings of the aristocracy, education was essentially limited to its members. Illiteracy was rampant, children were exploited by emerging industries, and the living conditions of the city workhouses were abominable. Yet, in this context Charles avers that the people who may be illiterate and who live in squalor have a "larger degree of confidence than the rich and learned." Of course, Charles's journal was not published in his own day, so that his posture in this matter had to emerge in other ways.

In these words from Charles's *MSJ*, one discovers a fundamental view of the psyche of the poor—in spite of their adverse living and labor

---

1 *MSJ*, 1:123.

2. Charles's sister Mehetabel.

3. *MSJ*, 1:123.

conditions and their lack of education, they are imbued with more confidence than the wealthy and well educated. David Lowes Watson maintains: "The truth of the matter is that God's deepest truths *are* grasped most readily by the poor, because they are the ones whose eyes God chooses to open. They are the ones who, lacking most worldly riches, are blessed with spiritual wealth."[4] Could this be the reason why Charles calls the poor his best friends?

In the year 1745, Charles gives an account of an accident he had while fleeing a mob at Shepton Mallet on August 10.[5]

> Preached at Shepton Mallet, where a great door is opening, and there are many adversaries. One of the devil's drunken champions attempted to disturb us, but my voice prevailed.
>
> They desired me to meet their little Society at an unusual place, to disappoint the mob. I walked forward toward the town, then turned back over the field, to drop the people, and, springing up a rising ground, sprained or broke my leg. I knew not which, but I fell down when I offered to set my foot to the ground. The brethren carried me to an hut, which was quickly filled with the poor people. It was soon noised about the town that I had broke my leg—some said my neck—and that it was a judgment upon me. The principal man of the place, Mr. P., sent me a kind message, and his bath-chair to bring me to his house. I thanked him, but declined his offer, on account of my pain, which unfitted me for any company except that of my best friends—the poor. With these I continued praying, singing, and rejoicing for two hours. Their love quite delighted me. Happiest they that could come near to do anything for me. When my strength was exhausted, they laid me on their bed, the best they had. But I could not sleep for pain.

In this incident Charles reveals that he declined the assistance of a man of means and chose to stay with the poor people who had assisted him and were caring for him, for he considered them to be his "best friends." This was very early in his ministry, just seven years after his conversion, and, although he certainly made friends among the wealthy and well educated, he does not seem to have changed his posture of claiming the poor as his best friends.

Friendship with the poor and marginalized is foundational for any relationship with them. It is much easier, however, to be a beneficent giver

4. Meeks, *Portion of the Poor*, 128.

5. *MSJ*, 2:445.

to the poor than it is to establish friendships. If one simply provides resources for the less fortunate, one can keep them at a distance. Friendship
means getting involved with others, their emotions and their behavior,
and the creation of mutual trust. Charles Wesley understood the value of
friendship as fundamental in his outreach to the poor.

AN ADVOCATE FOR THE POOR

The *MSJ* provides an account that reveals that Wesley was more than just
a friend to the poor. He was an advocate for them with civil authority at
Worcester after a mob attack.

> **Friday, July 5.** Between six and seven set out with Sarah Perrin,
> my wife, and sister Becky, and honest Francis Walker. Coming to
> Worcester in the afternoon, we heard the rioters had been at the
> room on Monday evening, in expectation of me, and made great
> disturbance. I doubted all along whether I had any business here
> at this time. Yet, at the desire of the poor people, went to their
> room at seven. Almost as soon as I began the mob interrupted.
> But in spite of their lewd, hellish language, I preached the gospel,
> though with much contention. They had no power to strike the
> people as usual, neither did any molest us in our way home.
>
> **Saturday, July 6.** We were hardly met, when the sons of Belial[6]
> poured in upon us, some with their faces blacked, some without
> shirts, all in rags. They began to "stand up for the Church," by
> cursing and swearing, by singing and talking lewdly, and throw-
> ing dust and dirt all over us; with which they had filled their
> pockets, such as had any to fill. I was soon covered from head
> to foot, and almost blinded. Finding it impossible to be heard, I
> only told them I should apply to the magistrates for redress, and
> walked up stairs. They pressed after me, but Mr Walker and the
> brethren blocked up the stairs, and kept them down. I waited a
> quarter of an hour, then walked through the midst of them to my
> lodgings, and thence to the mayor's.
>
> I spent an hour with him, pleading the poor people's cause.
> He said he had never before heard of their being so treated—that
> is pelted, beat, and wounded, their house battered, and windows,
> partitions, locks broke; that none had applied to him for justice,
> or he should have granted it; that he was well assured of the
> great mischief the Methodists had done throughout the nation,
> and the great riches Mr Whitefield and their other teachers had

6. See 1 Sam 2:12.

acquired; that their societies were quite unnecessary, since the Church was sufficient; that he was for having neither Methodists nor Dissenters.

I easily answered all his objections. He treated me with civility and freedom, and promised, at parting, to do our people justice. Whether he does or not, I have satisfied my own conscience.[7]

This is a very different view of Charles Wesley than is often found in the *MSJ*. Here he is in the midst of a mob attack, covered from head to foot with the dust and dirt that has been thrown at the poor people. Ironic, indeed, is the comment that the mob began "to 'stand up for the Church,' by cursing and swearing, by singing and talking lewdly, and throwing dust and dirt all over us." While he does not say this was a Society meeting, it was no doubt a group of poor people who were affiliated in some manner with the Methodist movement. Charles spoke up and announced that he would appeal to the local magistrates for redress. Though the mob pressed upon him when he started up the stairs, he was protected by some of the poor people, who blocked the mob's way. After a brief period, Charles mustered the courage simply to "walk through the midst of them" to his lodgings, and then proceeded to the mayor's.

Charles then pled the cause of the poor people before the mayor, who said that he had never heard of such behavior toward the poor. Though he was opposed to the Methodists, he promised that he would see that they were treated with justice. The account in the *MSJ* reveals that civil disobedience evoked a significant exercise of civil responsibility from Charles Wesley, who advocated on behalf of the poor before the local mayor because of the unjust attack on them.

RELATING TO THE POOR AND MARGINALIZED

There are a variety of clues in the *MSJ* as to how Charles related to the poor: (a) conversation, (b) worship, (c) prayer, (d) preaching, (e) invitation, and (f) Holy Communion. In addition, he reveals how his relationships with the poor impact his own life: (g) Charles Wesley's well-being, and (h) Charles Wesley's creativity.

Before addressing these aspects of Charles's life among the poor and marginalized, it is important to consider the encounter with "Justice Cr—, the most forward of our adversaries," as Charles records in the *MSJ*. This

7. *MSJ*, 2:611–12.

particular incident provides insight into the breadth of Charles's concern for the transformation of the life of the poor and its impact on the individual, family, and society.

> **Sunday, September 20 [1741].** Most of the Society were at St James's sacrament.
>
> I carried Mr Jones to Kingswood where the Lord was mightily present in his own ordinance. At Baptist Mills I expounded the bloody issue. Great disturbance was made behind me, till I turned upon the disturbers, and by the law first, and then the gospel, entirely silenced them.
>
> It was a glorious time at the Society, when God called forth his witnesses. Our guest was filled with consolation and acknowledged that God was with us of a truth.
>
> Introduced him to the leaders of the colliers with whom he had sweet fellowship. Met the bands and strongly urged them to press toward the mark. Read them a letter full of threatenings to take our house by violence. Immediately the power came down and we laughed all our enemies to scorn. Faith saw the mountain full of horsemen and chariots of fire. Our brother from Wales was compelled to bear his testimony and declare before all, what God had done for his soul. "At that time, when the power of the Holy Ghost so overshadowed him," (he assured them) "all bodily sufferings would have been as nothing. Neither would they feel them, if made partakers of the Holy Ghost in the *same measure*."
>
> He warned us to prepare for the storm, which would surely fall upon us, if the work of God went on. His artless words were greatly blessed to us all, and our hearts were bowed and warmed by the Spirit of love, as the heart of one man.
>
> **Tuesday, September 22.** He would have carried me to some great friends of his in the city, and particularly to a Counselor, about the threatened seizure. I feared nothing but helping myself and trusting to an arm of flesh. Our safety is to sit still. However, at his importunity I went with him a little way, but stopped and turned him back, and at last agreed to accompany him to Justice Cr—, the most forward of our adversaries.
>
> He received us cautiously. I said, "I came to wait upon him, in respect to his office, having heard his name mentioned among some, who were offended at the good we did to the poor colliers, that I should be sorry to give any just cause of complaint and willing to know from himself, if such had been given, that many vile reports were spread, as if he should countenance the violence

of those who had seized Mr C's house and now threatened to take away the collier's school.

I caught up an expression he dropped, that it would make a good workhouse, and said,

[Wesley]: "It is a workhouse already."

[Justice]: "Aye, but what work is done there?"

[Wesley]: "We work the works of God, which man cannot hinder."

[Justice]: "But you occasion the increase of our poor."

[Wesley]: "Sir, you are misinformed. The reverse of that is true. None of our Society is chargeable to you, even those who were so before they heard us, or who spent all their wages at the alehouse, now never go there at all, but keep their money to maintain their families, and have to give to those that want. Notorious swearers have now only the praise of God in their mouths. The good done among them is indisputable. Our worst enemies cannot deny it. None who hears us continues either to swear or drink."

[Justice]: "If I thought so," he hastily replied (*in eodem luto haesitans*[8]), "I would come and hear you myself."

I desired he would, said, the grace of God was as sufficient for him as for our colliers, and who knew but he might be converted among us![9]

It is generally known that there was opposition to the Wesleyan movement within the Church of England[10] and among certain institutional structures and government officials. On this occasion, Charles tells the justice that he has "heard his name mentioned among some, who were offended at the good we did to the poor colliers." He is curious whether the justice would sanction the seizure of Mr. Cennick's house and the taking away of the school for coal miners' children.

The justice maintains that the work the Wesleys and their followers are doing increases the poor. Charles then explains that precisely the reverse is occurring. He enumerates the changes that have transpired among the poor: (1) they no longer spend all of their wages at the alehouse; (2)

---

8. "Stuck in the same mud," Terence, *Phormio*, 780, though the original text reads *in eodem luto hesitas*.

9. *MSJ*, 1:333–35.

10. See Heitzenrater, *Wesley and the People Called Methodists*, 132–33, 170–71, 164. "Opposition continued in many forms, including the familiar mobs of hecklers and stone-throwers. Occasionally, the church people would amplify their displeasure by other means. For example, the church wardens in Pocklington hired men to ring the church bells while Wesley was preaching in the nearby street" (ibid., 202). See also *MSJ*, 2:388.

they use their money to sustain their families; (3) they give to others in need; (4) they no longer swear but instead praise God; and (5) they abstain from drinking. Wesley casts this work in a theological framework when he says to the justice, "We work the works of God, which man cannot hinder." In this conversation, however, the emphasis is not on the evangelical thrust of the Wesleyan movement, but rather its personal and societal impact. While the end result may be that the poor rise above the poverty line by using their meager resources for the sustenance of life and family and for others in need, this was not the primary goal as such of Wesleyan outreach. As will become obvious later in this study, in terms of Charles's fulfillment of the mandate to preach the gospel to the poor, he is fully convinced that by committing one's life to Christ and following in his way, not only will an individual life be transformed, but there will be a definitive impact on society. Charles's concern is for changed life and changed lives. Self-indulgence is transformed into caring concern for family and others.

Conversation

Charles Wesley understood that if you wish to establish a relationship with others, you must be willing to spend time conversing with them. As a well-educated graduate of Westminster School (London) and Christ Church College, Oxford University, how could he possibly build close relationships with persons who were poor and illiterate? He had read the great Latin and Greek poets; the uneducated would probably not even know who they were. He was a cleric of the Church of England, and many of the poor had perhaps never been inside a parish church. Charles knew that he had to spend time simply talking with those who were less fortunate than he was, if he wanted to relate to them.

On September 12, 1739, he wrote in the *MSJ*: "This conference abated my headache. Expounding at the Hall gave me more strength. After talking two hours with the poor people that came to me, and preaching at Baptist Mills, I was perfectly well."[11] Though there are a number of elements to be discussed in these three sentences, the focus here is on Charles's conversing for two hours with the poor people who came to him. While attending a conference, expounding at the Hall, and preaching at Baptist Mills, he takes time to talk with the poor for two hours. We do not know what he discussed with them, but we know that enduring relationships often develop when persons take time to converse with one another.

11. *MSJ*, 1:198.

No matter how important one thinks the other elements of the evangelical movement of the Wesleys may be, especially in terms of outreach among the poor and marginalized, Charles exemplifies a seminal aspect of lasting relationships: conversation.

A similar reference occurs in the *MSJ* on May 12, 1740: "Employed three hours most profitably in conferring with the poor people; more of whom daily receive forgiveness, or the witness of the Spirit. Three or four were now set at liberty, in immediate answer to prayer."[12] Here Charles spent yet a longer period of time in conversation with the poor. Again, while we do not know what he discussed with them, apparently faith-related issues were involved since he speaks of those who received forgiveness and the witness of the Spirit and were "set at liberty."

Regardless of the content of the conversation and the extent to which it was actually a dialogue between Charles and the poor, he sets an example for all who would minister among the poor: take time to converse with them.

Worshipping Together

Perhaps one of the least likely places to encounter the poor during the time of the Wesleys was the parish church, and among the least likely places to encounter priests of the Church of England were the workhouses, the hovels of the poor, and the hearths of Newcastle. In spite of the deep devotion of John and Charles Wesley to the Book of Common Prayer (BCP) and its liturgies, they understood that those least familiar with its words might better be introduced to the worship of God through singing, prayer, and preaching. They did not consider a less formal use of these elements of worship to be a substitute for the liturgies of the church, but they used them to engage the poor, illiterate, and others in the first steps of a journey toward a life in Christ and the church.

In the earliest stages of the Wesleys' ministry after their return from America, Charles records in the *MSJ* (June 6, 1739): "Above sixty of the poor people had passed the night in Mr Delamotte's barn, singing, and rejoicing. I sang and prayed with them before the door."[13]

In the *MSJ* passage cited earlier in this study in which Charles speaks of the poor as his best friends, he says, "With these I continued praying,

---

12. *MSJ*, 1:256.
13. *MSJ*, 1:176.

singing, and rejoicing for two hours."[14] These were indeed not times of formal worship in the sense of the liturgies of the BCP, though given the way in which the Wesleys' worship, prayer, and devotional life were rooted in the BCP, no doubt its phraseology and theology were integral to their articulation of faith in such gatherings. Of course, Charles integrated them into his hymns as well.[15]

Prayer

Prayer is, of course, a vital part of worship and devotional life. Wesley notes in the *MSJ* instances in which he spent time in prayer with the poor and marginalized outside the context of either formal or informal worship.

The first entry in the *MSJ* in which Wesley states that he spent time in prayer with poor people is dated Monday, September 4, 1738, not quite four months after his conversion on May 21st: "Charles Kinchin, now my inseparable companion, accompanied me to Bexley and Blendon. I prayed, and was comforted with the poor people." This experience brought solace to him. Presence among the poor and marginalized and prayer with them were a source of consolation. This would continue throughout Charles's life and ministry.

On February 19, 1739, he records:

> Prayed in the prison with Anne Dodd, well disposed, weary of sin, longing to break loose. Preached powerfully on the last day. Prayed after God for the poor harlots. Our sisters carried away one in triumph. I followed to Mrs Hanson's, who took charge of the returning prodigal. Our hearts overflowed with pity for her. She seemed confounded, silent, testifying her joy and love by her tears only. We sang and prayed over her in great confidence.[16]

Charles says that in prison he prayed with Anne Dodd. He does not say she is a prisoner, but one assumes that she was. He prayed as well for the prostitutes, one of whom, according to his account, "seemed confounded" and bore witness to "her joy and love by her tears." He goes on to say that they "sang and prayed over her in great confidence."

On May 7, 1740, Charles prayed with condemned prisoners: "God put it into our hearts to pray for the poor malefactors passing to

14. *MSJ*, 2:445.

15. See, for example, his hymnic response to the Great Litany in *Resurrection Hymns* (1746), Hymn 7, 10.

16. *MSJ*, 1:162.

execution; and his Spirit made intercession. I am sure (how much more the rest of us!) that our prayer was heard, and answered, upon some of our dying brethren."[17] Wesley regularly visited inmates of prisons, but in this instance they are condemned to death and are about to be executed. Wesley was convinced that the Spirit of God had made intercession for them and that prayer was effectual for some of those about to die. One assumes that his intercession for the condemned included the plea that they would commit their lives totally to God's care at this moment of trial.

A third reference to prayer with the poor and marginalized is found in the *MSJ* on April 4, 1745:

> Rode to Coleford, a place of colliers lately discovered, and preached in the church-yard on a tombstone. The church would not have contained a quarter of the congregation. I pointed them to "the Lamb of God, who taketh away the sin of the world" [John 1:29]. The poor people followed me to Mr Flowers's, where we wrestled two or three hours in prayer, and would not let him go, except he blessed us.[18]

Here the reference is to an extended period of prayer lasting from two to three hours. After preaching in the churchyard in Coleford, he went to the dwelling of Mr. Flowers and was followed by a group of poor people with whom he prayed.

Once again Charles Wesley's action is exemplary for the church—he *took time to pray* with the poor, prisoners, and prostitutes. While this may not have been a common practice of Anglican clergy in the eighteenth century, the Wesley brothers and the Methodist movement they initiated within the Church of England sought to follow the example of Christ and the mandate of Scripture to minister to the poor and marginalized.

Charles noted in the *MSJ*, however, that the power of prayer was not limited to his leadership. His record of November 6, 1744, states: "Expounded Acts 3 at Biddick, and found much life among this poor people. Many of them received forgiveness, chiefly under the prayer of one of the brethren raised up to serve them."[19]

17. *MSJ*, 1:253.

18. *MSJ*, 2:438.

19. *MSJ*, 2:426.

Preaching the Gospel

At the heart of Charles's motivation to proclaim the gospel to the poor and marginalized is the statement from the Gospel of Luke that he mentions in the *MSJ* entry for Sunday, March 30, 1740: "In the pulpit I opened the book on, 'The Spirit of the Lord is upon me, because the Lord hath anointed me to preach the gospel to the poor' [Luke 4:8]. I described our Lord's prophetic office, and the persons on whom *alone* he could perform it. We returned from the altar with the voice of praise and thanksgiving, among such as keep holiday."[20]

There are a number of citations in the *MSJ* that specifically identify the preaching of the gospel to the poor.

> **Tuesday, April 8** [1740]. Preached at the Common to six thousand poor, maimed, halt, and blind. Glory to Him, who is with his messengers *always*![21]

> **Friday, May 2** [1740]. Preached the gospel at Wapping to the poor. Their groans and tears testified their inward affection.[22]

> **Wednesday, July 20** [1743]. Preached at Zunnor, one of Mr Symond's four parishes, which is come in, to a man, at the joyful news. Some hundreds of the poor people with sincerity in their faces, received me saying, "The kingdom of heaven is at hand, repent ye, and believe the gospel" [Mark 1:15].[23]

> **June 5** [1743]. Rode to Sandhutton. The poor people filled the house where I was. I showed them the way of salvation in the creditor and two debtors.[24]

> **December 5** [1746]. Preached the gospel to the poor at Spen, their spirit bearing me up. Next morning we had a double blessing, and diligently poured out our souls before the Lord.[25]

In the discussion of his poetry and of justice for the poor in chapter 3, one will find that Charles Wesley addresses this subject eloquently and often.

---

20. *MSJ*, 1:231.
21. *MSJ*, 1:238.
22. *MSJ*, 1:250.
23. *MSJ*, 2:360.
24. *MSJ*, 2:353.
25. *MSJ*, 2:484.

Invitation

Charles understood that it is one thing to preach the gospel to the poor and quite another to express the hospitality of the gospel to them. If at times they were simply ignored by the Church of England, its clergy and members—if at times they were refused the sacrament of Holy Communion by the clergy, as Charles notes in the *MSJ*—it was important that they be invited to share in the family of God.

On November 30, 1746, Wesley recorded in the *MSJ* his passion for offering such an invitation to the poor and marginalized: "Went out into the streets of Newcastle, and called the poor, the lame, the halt, the blind, with that precious promise, 'Him that cometh unto me, I will in no wise cast out' [John 6:37]. They had no feeling of the sharp frost, while the love of Christ warmed their hearts."[26]

Here Charles expressed an evangelism of hospitality that motivated him to go into the streets of the city offering Christ's love to all.

Holy Communion

For Charles Wesley, participation in Holy Communion was integral to the evangelical movement of the Methodists and essential to the life of the Christian and the church. He wrote a brief treatise[27] on its importance, and with his brother John devoted an entire book to the subject, *Hymns on the Lord's Supper* (1745). This meal of the Lord is the most important meal of which anyone can partake, for the body and blood of Christ nourish and sustain life as no other meal can. Furthermore, it is a meal for all who seek to follow Christ and be a part of the body of Christ, the church. The table of the Lord is the symbol of the church's true unity. It is there that all who partake of the meal discover the fullness of God's love and care. Therefore, in Charles's outreach to the poor, it is evident that the poor and marginalized are to be included at the Lord's table, though this was not a view shared by all in the eighteenth-century Church of England.

Note Charles's comments in the *MSJ* on Sunday, July 20, 1740: "Our poor colliers being repelled from the Lord's table, by most of the Bristol ministers, I exhorted them, notwithstanding, to continue daily with one accord in the temple; where the wickedest administrator can neither spoil the prayers, nor poison the sacrament. *These* poor sinners *have* ears to

---

26. *MSJ*, 2:483.
27. See Newport, *Sermons of Charles Wesley*, 280–86.

hear."[28] Wesley makes clear that poor coal miners have been excluded from Holy Communion by many of the clergy in Bristol. When he says "our poor colliers," he probably means those who have some affiliation with the emerging evangelical movement called "Methodists." To exclude the poor coal miners from the Lord's table would seem to spoil the prayers and poison the sacrament; however, Wesley says no one can do that, for it is God's sacrament.

There is another very explicit statement in the *MSJ* for Sunday, May 29, 1743, regarding the participation of the poor and marginalized in Holy Communion: "At Birstal called the poor and maimed, and halt and blind to the great supper. My Lord disposed many hearts, I doubt not, to accept the invitation. He shows me several witnesses of the truth, which they have even now received in the love of it. Had a blessed parting with the Society."[29]

In the study of Wesley's poetry in chapter 3, we shall discover his extension of the theme of the importance of the Eucharist in life and ministry with and among the poor and marginalized.

Charles Wesley's Well-Being

There are a few entries in the *MSJ* that indicate that the poor are an inspiration to Charles, lift his spirits, and somehow improve his well-being.

> **Sunday, June 5** [1743]. My soul was revived by the poor people at Chowden, and yet more at Tanfield, where I called to great numbers, "Behold the Lamb of God," etc. [John 1:29, 36]. To the Society I spoke words not my own. At Newcastle one just come from the sacrament received the seal of forgiveness among us.[30]

> **Sunday, February 25** [1739]. Faint and spent at Blendon, I revived by exhorting above two hundred of the poor.[31]

> **Sunday, January 28** [1739]. Preached on "the three states" at Bexley. Some went out of church: and more in the afternoon, while I expounded, "Woe is unto me, if I preach not the gospel" [1 Cor 6:19]. Quite spent; yet renewed my strength for the poor people at night.[32]

---

28. *MSJ*, 1:274.
29. *MSJ*, 2:349.
30. *MSJ*, 2:350.
31. *MSJ*, 1:163.
32. *MSJ*, 1:159–60.

Tuesday, September 12 [1739]. [The] conference abated my headache. Expounding at the Hall gave me more strength. After talking two hours with the poor people that came to me, and preaching at Baptist Mills, I was perfectly well.[33]

Wesley must have been inspired by the fact that at times hundreds of the poor, if not thousands, gathered to pray, sing, and hear his preaching. Though he seems to have struggled with his health throughout much of his life, he did not let this stand in the way of his witness to the poor, if he could possibly avoid it. The presence of the poor apparently raised his spirits and inspired him to overcome physical weakness.

Charles Wesley's Creativity

There are two interesting entries in the *MSJ* for February 19 and 20, 1739, that illustrate that Charles Wesley's poetic creativity was inspired by the marginalized of eighteenth-century society. In this instance it is a prostitute.

Monday, February 19. Prayed in the prison with Anne Dodd, well disposed, weary of sin, longing to break loose. Preached powerfully on the last day. Prayed after God for the poor harlots. Our sisters carried away one in triumph. I followed to Mrs Hanson's, who took charge of the returning prodigal. Our hearts overflowed with pity for her. She seemed confounded, silent, testifying her joy and love by her tears only. We sang and prayed over her in great confidence.

Tuesday, February 20. Waked full of concern for the poor harlot; began an hymn for her. At five I call[ed] on Miss Crisp; then on Mr Stonehouse, where I expounded the woman taken in adultery.[34]

The prostitute so consumed his thought that he began to write a hymn for her. Wesley wrote poems for the aristocracy—such as kings,[35] nobility,[36] and distinguished musicians[37]—but in this instance, he was motivated by a

33. *MSJ*, 1:198.

34. *MSJ*, 1:162.

35. "A Prayer for his Majesty King George," *Hymns for Times of Trouble and Persecution*, 19–20; "For the King of Prussia," *Hymns of Intercession for all Mankind*, No. 12.

36. "On the Prince of Wales," *MS Festivals*, No. 7; Baker, *Rep. Verse*, 258.

37. "On the Death of Mr. Lampe," *Funeral Hymns*, (1759), 30–1, Hymn 16. Lampe was a well known bassoonist, composer, and conductor, who in 1746 published the volume *Hymns on the Great Festivals and Other Occasions* with twenty-four of his own compositions for twenty-four Wesley hymns (twenty-three by Charles and one by his

poor prostitute, who was struggling to find faith and change the direction of her life. This inspires Charles to write a hymn for her. The year 1739 is very early in his writing career, as he appears on the scene of English sacred poetry in 1738.[38] In the years to come, he would write many hymns and sacred poems about individuals, especially women, many of whom were by no means of the aristocracy, but who embodied, in his view, many of the most important aspects of Christian living and witness. Were it not for his poems, little or nothing would be known about some of them.

---

brother Samuel). Charles Wesley also wrote two poems for George F. Handel: "Ode on Handel's Birthday, S. Matthias Day Febr[uary] 24," and "Written in Handel's Lessons"; see *Unpub. Poetry*, 3:381–82.

38. It is believed that the hymn Charles Wesley wrote on the occasion of his conversion in May 1738 was "Where shall my wondering soul begin?"

III. Poetry

As we approach a broad spectrum of Charles Wesley's poetry that addresses life and ministry with and among the poor, we shall speak of his theology as one of radical grace. The perspectives of his *MSJ* and sermons already discussed lay the foundation for the understanding of this concept.

Randy Maddox has provided a vitally important study of Wesleyan theology in his work *Responsible Grace: John Wesley's Practical Theology,* which is more strongly dependent on the works and thought of John Wesley than Charles, though the latter does have a role in his discussion. The word *radical* (meaning thorough, far-reaching, and fundamental) is used here in the sense that Charles Wesley's views on life with the poor form an inherent or fundamental part of the nature of his theology, which in large measure were not embraced by the church and which require radical action, if they are to be embodied in Christian behavior and practice.

Grace is a seminal word and concept for Wesleyan theology, and Maddox's volume provides one of the finest studies of the multiple dimensions of its meaning for the Wesleys. Richard P. Heitzenrater also offers a perceptive description of grace in *Orthodox and Wesleyan Ecclesiology*: "Grace is relational—it is God's relationship with us, his activity in our lives, grounded in his loving attributes directed toward us." He quotes John Wesley's explanation as follows: grace "means that power of God the Holy Ghost which 'worketh in us both to will and to do of his good pleasure.'"[1] Furthermore, says Heitzenrater, "Grace is God's presence (that is to say, power) active in our lives. God's presence is always experienced (felt) as power of some sort or other. . . . God's power can be experienced in a myriad of ways."[2]

The importance of grace as a pivotal concept is unquestionably borne out in Charles Wesley's poetry. God is the author and implementer of grace

1. Heitzenrater, "Wesleyan Ecclesiology," in Kimbrough, *Orthodox and Wesleyan Ecclesiology,* 124.

2. Ibid.

that is extended to *all* of humankind, and the church and its members are instruments of divine grace. God's grace does not become effectual in a vacuum. God's presence anticipates and evokes human response. This is the co-respondent tension of the God/human grace relationship. Maddox speaks of John Wesley's desire "to preserve a dynamic tension that could celebrate whatever God's *grace* has already made possible in our lives, without relinquishing our *responsibility* to put that grace to work in the new areas that God continually brings to our attention."[3]

An area that God continually brings to Charles's attention is life with and among the poor. It seems difficult for him to conceive of God's grace without an integrated understanding of the role of the poor. In a poem in which he reflects on Jeremiah 31:34 ("They all shall know me from the least unto the greatest"), one finds the fundamental beginning point of Charles's theology of radical grace.

> Not from the greatest to the least[4]
>> The saving word shall move,
> The poor are chosen first, and blest
>> With thine enriching love:
> Now let thy knowledge upwards spread,
>> 'Till all their Lord embrace,
> Thro' faith from sin forever freed,
>> Forever saved by grace.

What makes this radical grace? The world does not see the poor as "chosen first." This is a radical view for human society in any age. When one considers the amount of discussion in the synagogue and the church over the centuries about who are "the chosen," from Rabbi Akiba and his followers to John Calvin's view of "the elect," Wesley's simple and distilled comment, "The poor are chosen first," is indeed radical. In spite of the averments of Scripture, this is not the view generally espoused by the Jewish and Christian communities. Not only are the poor "chosen first," says Charles, they are blessed with God's enriching love. Unquestionably the activities of Jesus in the New Testament reflect his distinctive outreach to the poor and marginalized of society, and there are glimpses in the church's history of its understanding of the importance of emulating this

---

3. Maddox, *Responsible Grace*, 190.
4. *Scripture Hymns* (1762) 2:33, poem no. 1234.

dimension of his ministry. This was not a dominant perspective, however, in the eighteenth-century Church of England of which Charles was a part.

While Charles, with his brother John, espoused a view of the universal nature of God's grace[5]—that is, it extends to all humankind—he recognized the vital task of sharing the gospel message "'Till *all* their Lord embrace." Through faith in Christ Jesus, they shall be freed from sin and saved forever by grace. Charles takes his cue from the prophet Jeremiah, "They all shall *know* me from the least unto the greatest," when he says, "Now let thy knowledge upwards spread." The knowledge of what God has done for humankind in and through the divine Son Jesus Christ is crucial to the redemption of all. While such a view has historically been accepted and endorsed within the church, a perspective that has received far less acceptance and endorsement is the one we find at the heart of Charles's theology of radical grace: "the poor are chosen first" as the recipients of God's grace and love. This perspective is rooted in Holy Scripture, as Petros Vassiliadis explains:

> Right from the beginning in the infancy narratives [of Luke's Gospel], the poor and lowly were chosen for the great privileges of witnessing and participating in the mystery of the divine incarnation: a childless couple, Zachariah and Elizabeth, Mary and Joseph from the unknown Nazareth, poor shepherds from the countryside. The Hymn of Mary (Magnificat) makes a strong reference to the poor and a renunciation of the rich. Also the beatitudes clearly affirm actual poverty.[6]

Charles also connects the kenotic revelation of God with the poor through the divestment of divine majesty and God's coming to dwell on earth. His thoughts are precipitated by the question posed in 1 Kings 8:27, "But will God indeed dwell on the earth?":

1. He did: the King invisible,[7]
    Jehovah, once on earth did dwell,
        And laid his majesty aside:
    Whom all his heavens cannot contain,

---

5. Universal grace should not be understood, however, as universal salvation without the need for repentance of sin.

6. Vassiliadis, *Eucharist and Witness*, 94. He suggests further, "Cf. also . . . the parable of the rich man and Lazarus (Luke 16:19–31) and the parable of the rich fool (12:13–21)."

7. *Scripture Hymns* (1762) 1:167, poem no. 533.

> For us he lived, a mournful man,
>> For us a painful death he died!

> 2. Still the great God resides below,
>> (And all his faithful people know
>>> He will not from his church depart)
>> The Father, Son, and Spirit dwells,
>> His kingdom in the poor reveals,
>>> And fills with heaven the humble heart.

Here too we encounter radical grace—the kingdom of God is revealed in the poor. How seriously has the church taken this to heart over the centuries? Of course, there are those servants—such as St. Francis of Assisi, Mother Teresa, and Martin Luther King Jr.—who have seen this vision clearly and who have given their lives for the poor.

For Charles Wesley *kenosis* is the central focus of an understanding of the Incarnation and life and ministry with the poor: God "laid his majesty aside." The Holy Trinity comes to dwell with humankind and reveals God's kingdom in the poor. This is a radical affirmation by Charles in stanza 2 of the poem cited above, but he is simply underscoring the claim of Holy Scripture. Divine Incarnation, the divine revelation *par excellence,* is intimately related to the poor, who are integral to God's revelatory process. They are channels of God's kingdom on earth.

It is not surprising that Wesley sees an important parallel in God's self-humbling baseness and poverty in the Incarnation, which he emphasizes in the following lines.

> Triumph we, the sons of grace,[8]
>> That our God is born so poor,
> Doth his majesty abase
>> Our salvation to secure.

In a poem based on John 6:24 ("When the people saw that Jesus was not there, they came to Capernaum, seeking for Jesus"), which remained unpublished at Charles's death, he emphasizes once more the revelation of God's kingdom through the poor.

> Come let us anew,[9]
>> Our Saviour pursue,

8. *Unpub. Poetry,* 2:79, poem based on Luke 2:7, stanza 3, lines 1–4.
9. *Unpub. Poetry,* 2:239.

Though now out of sight
We shall find him again, if we seek him aright.
　　Us who often has fed
　　With spiritual bread,
　　Will his comforts restore
And his kingdom brings in to the diligent poor.

　　Invisibly near,
　　He will quickly appear,
　　No more to depart,
In his Spirit he comes to abide in our heart;
　　Then united in love
　　His fullness we prove,
　　In his presence remain,
And never lose sight of our Saviour again.

GOD'S CHOSEN PEOPLE: THE POOR

Charles Wesley is very clear that the poor are God's chosen people, indeed a radical view over against the theologies of "the chosen" people often espoused by interpreters of the Hebrew and Greek Scriptures. He says:

The poor I to the rich prefer[10]
　　If with thine eyes I see;
To bear thy Spirit's character
　　The poor are chos'n by thee.
The poor in every age and place
　　Thou dost, O God, approve
To mark with thy distinguished grace,
　　To enrich with faith and love.

Who willingly affirms that the poor bear the character of the Spirit of God? Charles Wesley does. Then he says that no matter the time or place, the poor throughout all ages are marked by God's distinguished grace and are enriched with faith and love. Though these words of Wesley were not published during his lifetime, one wonders how would they have resonated with the Church of England, its bishops and clergy, and British society as a whole? Wesley avers that the poor people in the squalor of workhouses were marked by God's distinguished grace. This is something that most

---

10. *Unpub. Poetry*, 2:90. Charles is responding to Luke 4:26: "Unto none of them was Elias sent, save unto a woman that was a widow." Line 4 "chos'n" originally "chose."

clergy and church authorities did not acknowledge. As Charles says in the following poem, the poor are denied by the great and learned.

He stresses yet again the poor as "the chosen" people of God:

> God hath chose the simple poor,[11]
>   As followers of his Son,
> Rich in faith, of glory sure,
>   To win the heavenly crown:
> Him the vulgar still embrace
>   By the great and learned denied,
> Scorned by all the foes of grace,
>   And daily crucified.

How radical is the comment that if you scorn the poor, you are a foe of grace!

In another poem Wesley avers that the poor are Christ's followers, disciples, friends, and chosen witnesses.

> The poor, we joyfully confess[12]
>   His followers and disciples still,
> His friends, and chosen witnesses,
>   Who know his name, and do his will,
> Who suffer for our Master's cause,
> And only glory in his cross.

Charles anticipates that among the poor are those who indeed know Christ's name and do his will and even suffer for his cause.

When he reads the familiar verse, "You have the poor always with you" (Matt 26:11), he does not see this as a mere description of social reality. He understands the poor as having a specific role in the community of faith and a special relationship to Christ.

> The poor supply thy place,[13]
>   Deputed, Lord, by thee,
> To exercise our grace,
>   Our faith and charity,

---

11. *Unpub. Poetry.*, 2:240. Charles is responding to John 7:31: "Many of the people believed him."

12. *Scripture Hymns* (1762), 2:251, Hymn no. 433, stanza 2, based on John 7:48: "Have any of the rulers, or the Pharisees believed on him?"

13. Ibid., 2:189, Hymn no. 244.

And what to thee in them is given,
Is laid up for ourselves in heaven.

The poor have been appointed ("deputed") by Christ as those who "exercise our grace, / Our faith and charity." What can this mean? Has Christ appointed the poor to be poor, to live in squalor, to be poverty stricken, and always to be yearning for food, shelter, and clothing? Charles's use of the first person plural pronoun "our" is most interesting. How can the poor exercise *our* grace, faith, and charity? Are the poor essential to the exercise of the Christian's grace, faith, and charity? No. The poor, however, evoke the dynamism of the Christian's grace, faith, and charity. Apparently, Charles takes the Matthew verse at face value, namely, that the poor are a social reality, and Christ's followers must realize that their response to them is a response to Christ himself. They are as Christ in the world: "The poor supply thy [Christ's] place"—a radical view within the church and the world.

In another poem, instead of the verb "deputed," one finds the noun "deputies." It is based on Luke 18:22, "Yet lackest thou one thing."

One thing is lacking still[14]
But one which all implies,
To offer up thy heart and will,
And life in sacrifice;
With gladness to restore
Whate'er thy God hath given,
And thro' his deputies the poor
Lay up thy wealth in heaven.

Christ is God's evidence of grace, the free and unmerited divine love and salvation of sinners, in the world. If indeed, as Charles asserts, God's kingdom is revealed in the poor and they are God's deputies or appointees on earth, then to enfold them in the loving care of Christ's followers is a means by which grace, faith, and charity are dynamic forces in their lives. Wesley understands such action not as an option for Christian behavior, but rather as a mandate.

James 2:5, "Hath not God chosen the poor of this world?" is yet another biblical text that evokes Charles's close association of Christ and the poor. In the following poetical response to this biblical verse, his thoughts embrace Christ's own poverty and the challenge of divesting oneself of goods.

14. *Unpub. Poetry*, 2:171, MS Luke 266.

> Not many rich there are,[15]
>   Who choose thy poverty,
> Yet some are found, who dare
>   Sell all to follow thee:
> Jesus, thy blessed poor increase
>   To whom the kingdom's given,
> And let thy wealthy witnesses
>   Lay up their wealth in heaven.

Here, however, he mentions the rich and the fact that very few of them are willing to follow Christ's example of poverty. Yet, there are some who are willing to divest themselves of earthly goods to follow Christ. Wesley emphasizes again that the poor have been given the kingdom of God. When he prays in line 5 for the increase of the "blessed poor," this suggests that he is praying for the increase of the kingdom. Those who divest themselves of the wealth of the world choose the poverty of Christ and "Lay up their wealth in heaven."

In a tribute to Ebenezer Blackwell on the occasion of his death on April 23, 1782, Charles recalls someone who did not fully divest himself of earthly goods, but as a person of means continually aided the poor and thereby laid up treasures in heaven. Once again, Wesley equates giving to the poor with giving to God.

> Affliction's kind, unfailing friend,[16]
>   He wisely used his growing store,
> And priz'd his privilege to lend
>   To God, by giving to the poor:
> The Lord his lib'ral servant blessed,
>   Who paid him back the blessings given;
> And still, the more his wealth increased,
>   More treasure he laid up in heaven.

Rebekah Miles makes some remarks about John Wesley's emphasis on giving to the poor[17] that may also be applied to Charles: "The one example—giving to the poor—illustrates a larger point of Wesley's work.

---

15. *Scripture Hymns* (1762), 2:380, poem no. 740.

16. *Arminian Magazine* 6 (1783) 109, stanza 3, from the poem "On the Death of Mr. [Ebenezer] B[lackwell], who Died on Sunday, April 23, 1782."

17. See John Wesley's sermons: "The Danger of Increasing Riches," "The Use of Money," "The Danger of Riches," and "Causes of the Inefficacy of Christianity."

Christian moral action is a crucial component of our growth in holiness, or, in contemporary language, of our spiritual formation. Like prayer, moral living feeds our love for God and neighbor, while its absence leads to the deterioration of that love and the erosion of faith."[18] For Charles, as for John, there is a strong link between moral living and the path to holiness. Giving to the poor shapes our character and in a very positive way makes us more loving, which is essential to holiness.

In another text, Charles Wesley emphasizes the limited number of those who are willing to value the poverty of Christ. He reflects on the familiar passage from Luke's Gospel 9:57–58: "And it came to pass, that, as they went in the way, a certain man said unto him, 'Lord, I will follow thee whithersoever thou goest.' And Jesus said unto him, 'Foxes have holes, and birds of the air have nests; but the Son of man hath nowhere to lay his head.'"

1.   Saviour, how few there are[19]
        Who thy condition share,
    Few who cordially embrace,
        Love, and prize thy poverty,
    Want on earth a resting place,
        Needy and resigned like thee!

2.   I dare not ask thy pain
        And sorrow to sustain:
    But if thou vouchsafe me power
        Thee by want to glorify,
    Blessed with love I ask no more,
        Poor I live, and patient die.

Who of those who say they will follow Christ will love and prize his poverty? It is fine for the Son of God, the Savior, to have nowhere to lay his head, but who wants to live like that? Who wants to be homeless? Charles is aware that he cannot emulate all aspects of Christ's life, especially the pain of the cross and the Savior's sustained sorrow. He prays, however, that if God will empower him with the desire to glorify God, he will ask for nothing more than to be blessed with love, to be poor, and to die patiently. This is a radical prayer for a husband and father. Whether he can fully live in this manner is a question he poses to himself time and again. Yet, it is

18. Chilcote, *Wesleyan Tradition*, 109.
19. Charles Wesley, stanzas 1 and 2 from MS Luke, 144, in *Unpub. Poetry*, 2:115.

the honest desire of his heart. He treasures the blessing of God's love far more than earthly riches.

In a paraphrase of Psalm 131, he expresses his life perspective on the value of being "wean'd from every creature-good" so that nothing can supplant life in the happiness of love.

1. Lord, if thou the grace impart,[20]
   Poor in spirit, meek in heart,
   I shall as my Master be
   Rooted in humility.

2. From the time that thee I know,
   Nothing shall I seek below,
   Aim at nothing great or high,
   Lowly both my heart and eye.

3. Simple, teachable, and mild,
   Aw'd into a little child,
   Quiet now without my food,
   Wean'd from ev'ry creature-good.

4. Hangs my new-born soul on thee,
   Kept from all idolatry,
   Nothing wants beneath, above,
   Happy, happy in thy love.

5. O that all might seek and find,
   Every good in Jesus join'd,
   Him let Israel still adore,
   Trust him, praise him evermore!

Here one finds a life perspective on the acquisition of wealth that is at the heart of Charles Wesley's theology of radical grace: "Nothing wants beneath, above, / Happy, happy in thy love."

This perspective is punctuated further in his response to Acts 20:33, "I have coveted no man's silver, or gold, or apparel." His words reflect the tension between the desire for self-divestment and the desire not to judge the rich, a daily reality with which he lived.

The servant of a Master poor,[21]
Possessed of treasures that endure,

---

20. John and Charles Wesley, *Collection of Psalms and Hymns*, 95. This poem is unquestionably by Charles as confirmed by his manuscript collections.

21. *Unpub. Poetry*, 2:403.

> Can no terrestrial good desire,
> Silver, or gold, or gay attire;
> Nor will he judge who riches have,
> Limit th' Almighty's power to save,
> Or lump them with invidious zeal,
> And rashly send them all to hell.

This is indeed a delicate balance to achieve—to deprive oneself of all terrestrial goods, such as silver and gold and fancy attire, and at the same time to resist judging those who have such things. Humility is a hallmark of a theology of radical grace.

> Lord, if thou the grace impart,
> Poor in spirit, meek in heart,
> I shall as my Master be
> Rooted in humility.

INCLUSIVE LOVE

Time and again in Charles's poetry, one encounters his passionate understanding of the gospel message of inclusive love, which is seminal to his perspectives of justice for the poor. In *Redemption Hymns* (1747), he affirms the openness of God's love that embraces the marginalized of society.

> He hath opened a door[22]
> To the penitent poor,
> And rescued from sin,
> And admitted the harlots and publicans in:
> They have heard the glad sound,
> They have liberty found
> Thro' the blood of the Lamb,
> And plentiful pardon in Jesus's name.

The renewal of the human heart in commitment to Jesus Christ means an undying desire to model a life of love that includes everyone: "the penitent poor," harlots, and publicans. No one is excluded.

Matthew 22:10, "So those servants went out into the highways, and gathered together as many as they found, both bad and good: and the wedding was furnished with guests," inspires a poem that eloquently articulates God's inclusive love.

---

22. *Redemption Hymns* (1747), 4.

> God his grace on them bestows[23]
>   Whom he vouchsafes to call,
> No respect of persons knows,
>   But offers Christ to all:
> In the wedding-garment clad
> (The faith which God will not reprove)
> Poor and rich, and good and bad
>   May banquet on his love.

What a fascinating metaphor—all people, no matter their status in life (rich, poor, good, bad), may banquet on God's love. Having more or having less makes no difference. In God's realm there are no haves and have-nots. All are invited to the feast of God's love.

Wesley continues this poem and extends it to the Holy Eucharist:

> Many a bold, presumptuous guest,
>   Unholy and unfit,
> Share the sacramental feast,
>   And at this table sit.

Charles makes unequivocally clear that no one is excluded from this often most guarded and immured space of the church. The Lord's table is open to all. This is the feast of love in which all may participate, even the unholy and unfit!

Whom does Wesley mean when he says, "Many a bold, presumptuous guest, / . . . Share the sacramental feast"? Who are the presumptuous guests at the Lord's table? Without question, those who come to the table knowing they have excluded the poor are indeed presumptuous!

Nowhere is Wesley more articulate about the inclusive love he believes is central to the biblical message of redemption than in a lengthy poem titled "The Beatitudes. Matthew 5:3–12," which he published in his two-volume work *HSP* (1749).

> [95] Day and night thy ceaseless cries[24]
>   To the mercy-seat arise;
>   "Come, thou holy God and true!
>   Come, and my whole heart renew;

---

23. *Unpub. Poetry*, 2:37.

24. *HSP* (1749), 1:38–39, selected lines from the 162-line poem (No. 8) titled "The Beatitudes," based on Matt 5:3–12. Neither stanza nor line numbers appeared in the 1749 publication. Here the line number of the first line of each section of the poem appears in brackets.

Take me now, possess me whole,
Form the Saviour in my soul,
In my heart your name reveal,
Stamp me with thy Spirit's seal,
Change my nature into thine,
In me thy whole image shine:
Bow thine ear, in mercy bow,
Fill me with thy fullness now."

[109] Happy soul, who now renewed,
God in thee, and thou in God,
Only feel'st within thee move
Tenderness, compassion, love,
Love immense, and unconfin'd,
Love to all of humankind,[25]
Love, which willeth all should live,
Love, which all to all would give,
Love, that over all prevails,
Love, that never, never fails:
Stand secure, for thou shalt prove
All th' eternity of love.

. . .

[129] Happy soul, whose active love
Emulates the blest above,
In thy every action seen,
Sparkling from the soul within:
Thou to every sufferer nigh,
Hearest, not in vain, the cry
Of the widow in distress,
Of the poor and fatherless!
Raiment thou to all that need,
To the hungry deal'st thy bread,
To the sick thou giv'st relief,
Sooth'st the hapless prisoner's grief,
The weak hands thou liftest up,
Bid'st the helpless mourners hope,
Giv'st to those in darkness light,
Guid'st the weary wanderer right.

25. Charles Wesley uses both "mankind" and "humankind" in his poetry to describe all human beings collectively. Here he uses the latter word.

This lengthy poem might be used as a "litany of *theosis*" with a recurring congregational refrain of the lines, "Love immense and confined, / Love to all of humankind." In this text, Wesley rehearses what it means to participate in the divine nature, that is, for the Savior to be formed in one's soul. As emphatically as many of the Eastern Church Fathers,[26] he stresses over and over that human beings are made to share in the life or nature of the Holy Trinity. If the Savior is formed within one's soul, this means a radical change in one's life. Wesley articulates what he views as the enduring plea of all humankind in the lines, "Change my nature into thine, / In me thy whole image shine."

He then goes on to describe what it means when God is in you and you are in God: You are moved only by tenderness, compassion, and love. This love is immense and unlimited and embraces everyone throughout the earth. Such love wills life for all and does not fail. This, then, is how he sees the community of believers—a community empowered in and only through love for all.

The series of rhyming couplets on the limitless expanse of love are worthy of continual repetition by the followers of Christ. They are an eloquent articulation of the biblical understanding of love and its Wesleyan interpretation.

> Love immense, and unconfined,
> Love to all of humankind,
> Love, which willeth all should live,
> Love, which all to all would give,
> Love, that over all prevails,
> Love, that never, never fails:
> Stand secure, for thou shalt prove
> All th' eternity of love.

Wesley does not leave this "litany of *theosis*" in the abstract. Beginning with line 129, he moves to "active love" that is to be seen in human behavior. Here is what active love does: Hears the cries of distressed widows, the poor, and fatherless; gives clothes to the needy, food to the hungry, relief to the sick, comfort to the imprisoned, strength to the weak, hope to those in mourning, and light to those in darkness.

26. For example, Gregory of Nyssa and Ephrem Cyrus. See the discussions of Peter Bouteneff, "All Creation in United Thanksgiving," and Frances Young, "Inner Struggle," in Kimbrough, *Orthodox and Wesleyan Spirituality*, 189–204, 157–72. See also Allchin, *Participation in God*; Christiansen and Wittung, *Partakers of the Life Divine*; and Kimbrough, "Theosis in the Writings of Charles Wesley," 199–212.

In a similar manner, in two short poems of *Scripture Hymns* (1762), Wesley emphasizes the importance of *theosis*. He prays:

> Thou, Lord, of life the fountain art;[27]
> Oh could I find thee in my heart!

In another poem from the same volume, he prays:

> To me, for Jesu's sake, impart[28]
> And plant thy nature in my heart.

When the divine nature is planted in the human heart, the result is the active engagement of inclusive love, as the two stanzas that follow this couplet stress:

> Thy mind throughout my life be shown,[29]
>   While listening to the wretch's cry,
> The widow's and the orphan's groan,
>   On mercy's wings I swiftly fly,
> The poor and helpless to relieve,
> My life, my all, for them to give.
>
> Thus may I show thy Spirit within,
>   Which purges me from every stain;
> Unspotted from the world and sin
>   My faith's integrity maintain,
> The truth of my religion prove
> By perfect purity and love.

The evidence that one has the mind of Christ is that one listens to the wretch's cry. One does not simply hear the cry—one listens to it. In so doing, one moves swiftly out of compassion to relieve the poor and helpless. One makes the life-changing decision: "My life, my all, for them to give." As John Newton suggests, "Charles makes such compassion one of the supreme tests of whether a professing Christian really does have the Spirit of Jesus at work in his or her heart and life."[30]

---

27. Lines 5 and 6 of stanza 1 of the hymn "Jesus, the gift divine I know," *Scripture Hymns* (1762), 2:244, Hymn no. 413.

28. Lines 5 and 6 of stanza 1 of the hymn "Father, on me the grace bestow," *Scripture Hymns* (1762), 2:380, Hymn no. 739.

29. Ibid., stanzas 2 and 3.

30. Newport and Campbell, *Charles Wesley,* 66.

Those who have God's nature planted in their hearts willingly give their lives, their all, for the poor and helpless and thereby maintain the integrity of their faith. The truth of their religion is "perfect purity and love," which has no boundaries. They waste no time in relieving the poor and helpless—indeed, they fly on "mercy's wings" to aid them.

Active, inclusive love is a powerful witness with the ability to transform lives. In paying tribute to Elizabeth Blackwell[31] at her death, Charles holds up her life to the community of faith as exemplary of the power of this kind of love.

> Touching the legal righteousness,[32]
>   While blameless in thy sight she lived,
> Thee she confessed in all her ways,
>   And all her good from thee received;
> Faithful even then, she flew to tend,
>   Where'er distressed, the sick and poor,
> Rejoiced for them her life to spend,
>   And all thy gifts through them restore.
>
> . . .
>
> By wisdom pure and peaceable,[33]
>   By the meek Spirit of her Lord,
> She knows the stoutest to compel,
>   And sinners wins without the word:
> They see the tempers of the Lamb,
>   They feel the wisdom from above,
> And bow, subdued, to Jesu's name,
>   The captives of resistless love.
>
> . . .
>
> Her living faith by works was shown:
>   Through faith to full salvation kept,
> She made the sufferer's griefs her own,
>   And wept sincere with those that wept:

31. *Poet. Works*, 6:323–331; a lengthy four-part poem titled "On the Death of Mrs. Elizabeth Blackwell, March 27, 1772." For an incomplete manuscript version of the poem cf. the file "On the Death of Elizabeth Blackwell" on the Web site of the Center for Studies in the Wesleyan Tradition, http://www.divinity.duke.edu/initiatives-centers/cswt/wesley-texts/manuscript-verse.

32. Ibid., 324.

33. Ibid. 326–27. The following two stanzas are from Part II of the Elizabeth Blackwell poem, the latter of which does not appear in the manuscript version.

Nursing the poor with constant care,
Affection soft, and heart-esteem,
She saw her Saviour's image there,
And gladly ministered to him.

Why is Elizabeth Blackwell's active love so effective? Others see in her the tempers of Christ, Wesley says. They sense in her divine wisdom, and therefore they become captives of the resistless love she exhibits. Once again, Wesley does not leave one to wonder or speculate about how this might have transpired. He is very specific. She was able to make the griefs of others her own; she wept with those that wept. A key word, however, in the line about weeping is that her tears were "sincere." Hers was not a superficial identification with others' sorrows; it was deeply earnest.

"Her living faith by works was shown." She nursed the poor with constant care and realized that in ministering to the poor she was ministering to Christ. In the poor she saw the image of Christ. She rejoiced to spend her life for the poor and distressed.

Wesley saw evidence during his life and ministry of those who were the embodiment of God's inclusive love that is resistless when it is active in the lives of the faithful. Elizabeth Blackwell exemplified such love to the church and world in the eighteenth century. This kind of love needs no words, for she won sinners "without the word." They bow to Jesus' name, for they have been captivated by the love they have seen in her that they cannot resist.

Just as Elizabeth Blackwell identified Christ in the poor, so did Grace Bowen, according to Charles Wesley in stanzas 9 and 10 of his poem "On the Death of Mrs. Grace Bowen, January 2, 1755."[34]

She loved them both in word and deed,
O'erjoyed an hungry Christ to feed,
   To visit him in pain;
Him in his members she relieved,
And freely as she first received,
   Gave him her all again.

How did her generous bounty deal
The widow's scanty oil and meal,
   A treasure for the poor?
A treasure spent without decrease,
As miracle revived to bless
   The consecrated store.

34. *Funeral Hymns* (1759), 25.

What a marvelous example Grace Bowen was to others: she loved others in word and deed. When feeding the hungry, she was nurturing Christ; when visiting those in pain, she was comforting Christ. Once again, Wesley emphasizes the complete commitment of this woman: she "Gave him [Christ] her all again." Once more there is the mutual identification of Christ and the poor. Wesley employs the metaphor of the widow of Zarephath from 1 Kings 17, when he speaks of "The widow's scanty oil and meal." Even if Grace Bowen had meager nourishment to share, she generously offered it to the poor: "A treasure spent without decrease." All of this was an expression of her love for others, a love that did not exclude the poor.

Wesley articulates this most explicitly in a direct response to 1 Kings 17:16, "The barrel of meal wasted not, neither did the cruse of oil fail." The admonition is to all:

> That thy stock may never cease,[35]
> That thy little may increase,
> Gladly of that little give,
> Poor thyself, the poor relieve.

Even a person of meager means can aid the poor from that which he or she has.

Charles Wesley knew that justice for the poor was not possible without inclusive, selfless, active love as experienced in Jesus Christ and embodied in all aspects of one's behavior.

A POSTURE OF JUSTICE

In *Scripture Hymns* (1762), there is a quatrain based on Matthew 23:23 ("Ye have omitted the weightier matters of the law") that expresses Charles Wesley's life posture.

> May I, observant of the least,[36]
> Most careful in the greatest prove,
> And show throughout my life exprest
> Justice, fidelity, and love.

---

35. *Scripture Hymns* (1762), 1:170, Hymn no. 541.
36. Ibid., 2:182, poem no. 217.

Two words are extremely important in these four lines: "observant" and "show." Throughout his life Charles wants to make certain that he is quick to notice "the least." He wishes to be keenly aware of those who are less fortunate, and he wants to be very discerning with the fortunate. Above all, and for his entire life, he desires to demonstrate "Justice, fidelity, and love." This brief poem is a simple prayer worthy to be prayed daily by those who would live a life of radical grace. The trilogy of "justice, fidelity, and love" is an ethical complement to St. Paul's trilogy of "faith, hope, and love."

In *HSP* (1749) Charles penned a series of poems under the heading "Hymns for the Persecuted." Hymn II is titled "For the Brethren of Wednesbury."[37] He composed the poem in the first person plural as if the seven stanzas were the urgent prayers of persons who are being persecuted and oppressed. In the sixth stanza, Charles expresses a perspective that is fundamental to a theology of radical grace.

> Thou wilt not shut thy bowels up,[38]
>   Or justice to the opprest deny;
> Thy mercy's ears thou canst not stop
>   Against the mournful prisoner's cry,
> Who ever make our humble moan,
> And look for help to thee alone.

If God does not deny justice to the oppressed, then those in whom God's nature dwells must not withhold justice from them.

In another poem, Charles Wesley holds up to the community of faith the life of Mary Naylor as exemplary of a life that personified what it means to live an ethic of justice for others, particularly the poor. Here are selected stanzas from the lengthy poem that celebrates her life.

> The golden rule she has pursued,[39]
> And did to others as she would

---

37. Wednesbury, Staffordshire, was located six miles northwest of Birmingham. Charles visited Wednesbury a number of times to preach and minister to the coal miners. A Society of three hundred or so had been organized there, and it was under continual attack from mobs that opposed the Methodist movement.

38. *HSP* (1749), 2:111.

39. *Funeral Hymns* (1759), 49–53; the stanzas are from the lengthy poem "On the Death of Mrs. Mary Naylor, March 21st, 1757"; the first stanza is from Part II (original stanza 3), 51; the next three stanzas come from Part III (original stanzas 2–4), 53; the final stanza is from Part I (original stanza 2), 49–50. Original first line: The golden rule she still pursued.

Others should do to her:
Justice composed her upright soul,
Justice did all her thoughts control,
    And formed her character.

Affliction, poverty, disease,
Drew out her soul in soft distress,
    The wretched to relieve:
In all the works of love employed,
Her sympathizing soul enjoyed
    The blessedness to give.

Her Saviour in his members seen,
A stranger she received him in,
    An hungry Jesus fed,
Tended her sick, imprisoned Lord,
And flew in all his wants to afford
    Her ministerial aid.

A nursing-mother to the poor,
For them she husbanded her store,
    Her life, her all, bestowed;
For them she laboured day and night,
In doing good her whole delight,
    In copying after God.

Away, my tears and selfish sighs!
The happy saint in paradise
    Requires us not to mourn;
But rather keep her life in view,
And still her shining steps pursue,
    Till all return to God.

Charles's observation that justice composed Mary Naylor's soul, controlled her thoughts, and formed her character is a statement that captures in three lines of poetry what he envisions as the posture for all who claim the name of Jesus Christ. Is it possible to imagine a community of believers who actually live as this woman did? Wesley avers that Naylor's life is an affirmative answer to this question: it is possible to be consumed by the love of God so that justice controls all one is and does.

Interestingly, Charles says that "Affliction, poverty, disease, / *drew out* her soul in soft distress." She was not simply moved by this trilogy of human suffering, it *drew out* her soul. She became employed in works of love to relieve those who were in dire need. Mary Naylor clearly heeded the admonition of Charles's sermon on Titus 3:8, "Let it be your constant employment to serve and relieve your Saviour in his poor distressed members." In his tribute to her, he writes that she saw Christ in strangers and received them, in the hungry and fed them, in the sick and imprisoned and tended them. In aiding all of them, she was ministering to Christ.

Furthermore, Wesley says that she literally gave her life, her all, to be a nursing-mother to the poor. She labored for them day and night—"in doing good her whole delight, / in copying after God."

Wesley did not write this poem about Mary Naylor merely to pay tribute with eloquent words, but so that all may "keep her life in view" and pursue her shining steps "till all to God return." Thus, responding to the needs of others as she did is a form of evangelism, for it inspires people to return to God.

How then can one develop and maintain a vibrant posture of justice in one's life?

If one keeps Mary Naylor's life in view and walks in her steps, one will:

Step 1: pursue the golden rule: do to others as others should do to you;

Step 2: let your soul be drawn out by affliction, poverty, and disease;

Step 3: be continually employed in works of love;

Step 4: give your life, your all, for the poor, and work for them day and night;

Step 5: do not lose sight of steps 1–4.

THE CHURCH

Charles Wesley's view of the *catholicity* of the church is seminal to a theology of radical grace and justice for the poor. The church is the body of Christ and includes those who trust in him and have committed their lives to follow him. Nevertheless, Wesley anticipates a church that includes all of humankind.

> A church to comprehend[40]
> The whole of human race,

40. *Scripture Hymns* (1762), 1:392, poem no. 1160, based on Isa 66:21–23.

> And live in joys that never end
>> Before thy glorious face.

"The whole of human race" obviously embraces all human beings, including the poor. Unquestionably Wesley views the church as the unfragmented universal body of believers.

> One family we dwell in him,[41]
>> One church above, beneath,
> Though now divided by the stream,
>> The narrow stream of death.

In the midst of the eighteenth-century divisions of the church—various Protestants and Dissenters in Great Britain and on the European continent, factions and controversies within the Church of England (e.g., non-Jurors), Reformed and Lutheran Churches, Roman Catholic Church, etc.—Charles's vision of the church is one of unity that transcends any divisions.

> Many are we now and one,[42]
> We who Jesus have put on,
> There is neither bond nor free,
> Male nor female, Lord, in thee.

> Love, like death, hath all destroyed,
> Rendered all distinctions void:
> Names and sects, and parties fall,
> Thou, O Christ, art all in all.

Even so, Charles was aware that there were divisions in the church and in society and knew the gospel must be proclaimed to the poor. For him this is a self-understood dimension of the church's mission. Whoever has not come to know Christ, poor or wealthy, must hear the good news of the gospel. What he writes in his powerful hymn on the church's mission, "Give me the faith that can remove / The mountain to the plain," spells out a two-dimensional purpose for the church. *All* those who have committed their lives to Christ and the church are to do the following:

> To spend and to be spent for them[43]
>> Who have not yet my Saviour known,

41. *Funeral Hymns* (1759), hymn no. 1, stanza 2:1-4.
42. HSP (1740), 195.
43. HSP (1749), 1:301, stanza 5:4-6.

> Fully on these my mission prove,
> And only breathe, to breathe thy love.

Two things are evident from Charles's words: (1) There is a commitment to share the message of God's redemptive love in Christ with all who have not heard it. He does not articulate this merely as an obligatory verbal exercise. While he affirms time and again the importance of preaching the gospel to the poor, in these lines he is saying that one spends one's life—time, energy, resources—in order to share the gospel with those who have not heard it. (2) One must breathe for only one reason—to breathe the love of God.

Preaching

Unquestionably preaching the gospel to the poor is a priority for Charles Wesley. He mentions this more than once in letters to his wife, Sally. On April 5, 1760, he wrote to her: "From her [Miss Boys] we walked to Miss Shirley's, at Marybone. She carried us to a sick woman, who used to hear Mr. Whitefield. I found her dying without Christ, and preached pure Gospel to the poor. She believes he will come and save her: therefore she cannot die unsaved."[44] Here is an example of an intimate verbal sharing of the gospel; nevertheless, he says he "preached" to the woman.

On another occasion, he wrote the following to his wife:

> Sunday, September 3d. My text in the morning was, "In these is continuance, and we shall be saved." Almost all the Society met me at the Lord's table. The Minister administered to me first, as if he wanted to gain the hearts of our people. Our room was too narrow for us in the evening; so we borrowed the market-house, which is capable of holding thousands. Thousands attended gladly, while I explained and applied, "The poor have the Gospel preached to them" [Matt. 11:5]. My mouth was opened to make known the mystery of salvation by grace.[45]

In contrast to the previous communiqué to his wife, Charles records here preaching to thousands on the text "The poor have the Gospel preached to them." He does not say that he is preaching to the poor *per se*; rather, he shares with the throng that there is a mandate of Scripture that the gospel

---

44. Jackson, *Journal*, 2:231.
45. Ibid., 2:220.

is to be preached to the poor. Thus, the obligation falls not only to the clergy but to all followers of Christ.

Preaching the gospel to the poor is not, however, a simplistic matter. It has a deep impact on the proclaimer or preacher. Charles writes about this in a poem that was not published during his lifetime. It is a personal testimony to the effect that such proclamation has on the one delivering the message.

1. While preaching gospel to the poor,[46]
   My soul impoverish and secure
      By deep humility;
   Safe in your wounds a novice hide,
   Then shall I preach the Crucified,
      And nothing know but thee.

2. Here may I covet no reward,
   No trifles temporal regard,
      Or reckon earth my home,
   But things invisible desire,
   And wait for my appointed hire
      Till the great Shepherd come.

3. A life of poverty and toil,
   A thousand lives, one gracious smile
      Of yours will overpay,
   If thou receive me with "Well done!"
   And for thy faithful servant own,
      In that triumphant day.

In the first stanza, Wesley is clear that preaching the gospel to the poor evokes humility. This is indeed a radical prayer—to pray that God will impoverish your soul and make you secure in deep humility—but that is what he prays. He is very self-effacing when in line 4 of stanza 1 he speaks of himself as a novice. Only from this posture, Charles avers, is one prepared to "preach the Crucified." Nothing should become an obstacle to the singular focus of preaching the Crucified.

The remaining two stanzas further emphasize the spirit of humility. He says, "Here may I covet no reward," and he desires only "invisible things."

---

46. MS Preachers 1786, 9–10; in *Unpub. Poetry*, 3:49; stanzas 2, 5, and 6 (of six stanzas).

The preacher of the gospel, however, usually desires tangible results. In the third stanza, Wesley takes his analogy of humility to its extreme when he says that even if he should be destined to a life of poverty and toil and a thousand lives be gained, God's acknowledgment in the day of triumph with "Well done!" will be an overpayment for his ministry to the poor.

Here is a key to preaching the gospel to the poor: it must be done with the deepest possible sense of humility in order to be effective. Charles emphasizes this further when responding to Matthew 11:5, "The poor have the gospel preached to them."

> Prepared by sacred poverty,[47]
> Jesus, the power of God in me
>   Unto salvation prove,
> Preach to my troubled soul thy peace,
> Inspire with all thy holiness,
>   With all thy heavenly love.

Wesley does not talk about the task of preaching *per se*, but rather about the importance of being prepared for the task by "sacred poverty." Before he preaches to anyone else, he asks that God preach peace to his troubled soul and inspire him with holiness and love.

After preaching to the colliers at Newcastle, Wesley gives God all the praise for any effectiveness of his preaching to the poor and writes the following:

> 1.   Glory to Christ be given[48]
>   By all in earth and heaven!
> Christ, my prophet, priest and King,
>   Thee with angel-quires I praise,
> Joyful hallelujahs sing,
>   Triumph in thy sovereign grace.

> 2.   Thou hast the hungry filled,
>   Thou hast thy arm revealed;
> Thou in all the heathen's sight,
>   Hast thy righteousness displayed,
> Brought immortal life to light,
>   Ransom'd whom thy hands have made.

---

47. *Scripture Hymns* (1762), 2:160, poem no. 135.

48. *HSP* (1749), 1:312, 314, poem no. 332, stanzas 1, 2, 3, and 12 (of thirteen stanzas).

3.   Ev'n now, all-loving Lord,
          Thou hast sent forth thy word,
  Thou the door hast opened wide
      (Who can shut thy open door!)
  I the grace have testified,
      Preached thy gospel to the poor.

. . .

12.   Still let me preach thy word
         The prisoner of the Lord
  Fully my commission prove,
      'Till the perfect grace I feel,
  Saved and sanctified by love,
      Stamp'd with all thy Spirit's seal.

The Clergy

As concerned as Charles Wesley is for the preaching of the gospel to the poor, he is equally concerned with the ministers who proclaim the gospel message. What is their attitude toward the poor? Are they mediators of God's justice among the poor? Are they more concerned with themselves than with others? After reading chapter four of the Acts of the Apostles, he wrote some keenly perceptive lines about the commitment of the clergy that unfortunately were not published in his lifetime. His poem was precipitated by Acts 4:36–37, "And Joses, who by the apostles was surnamed Barnabas, (which is being interpreted, the son of consolation,) a Levite, and of the country of Cyprus, having land, sold it, and brought the money, and laid it at the apostles' feet."

1. Ye Levites[49] hired who undertake[50]
    The aweful ministry
  For lucre or ambition's sake,
    A nobler pattern see!
  Who greedily your pay receive,
    And adding cure to cure,
  In splendid ease and pleasures live
    By pillaging the poor.

49. Clearly Wesley intends "Levites" to mean the priests/pastors of his day.

50. *Unpub. Poetry*, 2:298–99, MS Acts, 75.

2. See here an apostolic priest,
    Commissioned from the sky,
  Who dares of all vain self divest,
    The needy to supply!
  A primitive example rare
    Of gospel-poverty,
  To feed the flock one's only care,
    And like the Lord to be.

3. Jesus, to us apostles raise,
    Like-minded pastors give
  Who freely may dispense thy grace
    As freely they receive;
  Who disengaged from all below
    May earthly things despise,
  And every creature-good forego
    For treasure in the skies.

Chapter 4 of the book of Acts relates how believers in Christ respond to others in diverse contexts. The chapter opens with the arrest of Peter and John for speaking to the people in the temple concerning Christ's resurrection, and their appearance before the Jerusalem Council. The response of Peter and John before those who oppose them is to hold steadfast in the faith. Before the Council they boldly declare, "There is salvation in no one else, for there is no other name under heaven given among mortals by which we must be saved" (4:12).

After their release, they talk about their experiences with friends, who pray a moving prayer for boldness to speak God's Word. No doubt they are moved by the boldness of Peter and John. Peter had declared, "we cannot keep from speaking about what we have seen and heard" (4:20). Peter and John respond to their friends by joining with them in praise and prayer to God.

In this hymn, Wesley focuses on a specific response to others and human need: the selfless act of Barnabas, a priest of the lineage of Levi, who sold his land and brought the proceeds and presented them as a gift to the apostles. Wesley sees this action as exemplary for all who serve as pastors or ministers.

In the first stanza, Wesley states what the pastoral office is not and addresses all who undertake the vocation of ministry; he summons them to consider a nobler pattern for ministry than money and ambition. It may seem strange to hear an eighteenth-century poet-priest warning pastors that those who live in splendid ease and with the pleasures of life are living at the expense of others. But Wesley declares they are "pillaging the poor."

In the second stanza, Wesley states what the pastoral office is. He sees Barnabas as exemplary of one whose pastoral commission and vocation are truly from God. Yet, Wesley regards him as a rare example of self-divestment, as was Christ throughout his life and upon the cross. Wesley calls this "gospel poverty"—becoming poor for the sake of others and the gospel. Barnabas' only goal was "to feed the flock."

In stanza 3, Wesley prays a prayer that all pastors should continually pray. For what should they pray? To have a mind like Barnabas; to dispense God's grace as freely as they have received it; to become detached from earthly things; to be willing to forego the benefits of earthly existence, for the wealth of God's realm cannot be measured in earthly possessions.

Wesley emphasizes what the Scriptures say—the only thing we may keep is what we give away. Hence, self-divestment is the vocation of Christ's followers. It is the pastoral way of life.

While Wesley avers in the above poem that the clergy may pillage the poor through their self-serving behavior, in another poem, one based on Luke 20:14 ("Come, let us kill him, that the inheritance may be ours"), he suggests that priests who live in ease and pleasure kill the poor through negligence. They "eat, and drink, and sport their fill, / And let the poor thro' hunger die."

> Ambitious, covetous, and vain,[51]
>   Priests who in ease and pleasure live,
> They persecute their Lord again,
>   His members vex, his Spirit grieve;
> Souls by their negligence they kill,
>   Jesus afresh they crucify,
> And eat, and drink, and sport their fill,
>   And let the poor thro' hunger die.

The poem is based on the parable of the vineyard in Luke 20. The owner of the vineyard has traveled to a distant country, and three times he sends servants to procure fruit from the vineyard, but each time they are mistreated by the husbandmen who have been charged with tending the

---

51. *Unpub. Poetry*, 2:183, MS Luke, 288.

vineyard. Finally, the owner determines to send his son, and this is when those tending the vineyard consider killing him so that they somehow might possess the vineyard.

While Charles does not appropriate the complete parable in his poem, the line of the Lucan passage, "Come, let us kill him, that the inheritance may be ours," precipitates the thought that priests, who are supposedly tending the vineyard of the Lord—namely, the world in which they live, which is filled with the poor—are preparing themselves to kill God's own representatives, the poor, by neglecting them and by satisfying their own selfish desires. Thus, they let the poor die of hunger, and in so doing they crucify Christ again.

These are harsh words indeed, but for Charles they are a reality. As severe as are the aforementioned critiques of the clergy, perhaps his most scathing poetical indictment of the clergy is found in a poem based on Luke 20:46–47: "Beware of the scribes, who desire to walk in long robes, and love greetings in the markets, and the highest seats in the synagogues, and the chief rooms at feasts; which devour widows' houses, and for a show make long prayers: the same shall receive great damnation."

1. Alas for us, who need beware[52]
   Of men that sit in *Moses'* chair,
       And should to heaven the people guide!
   Men with the pomp of office clad,
   In robes pontifical arrayed,
       But stained with avarice and pride:
   They love to be prefered, adored,
   Affect the state and stile of *lord,*
       And shine magnificently great;
   They for precedency contend,
   And on ambition's scale ascend
       Hard-labouring for the highest seat.

2. The church they call their proper care,
   The temple of the Lord they are,
       Abusers of their legal power;
   Greedy the church's goods to seize,
   Their wealth they without end increase,

---

52. *Unpub. Poetry,* 2:186, MS Luke, 294–95. See also *Rep. Verse,* 306, no. 269. The first six lines of each stanza appear in *Poet. Works,* 11:275.

> And the poor widow's house devour.
> O what a change they soon shall know,
> When torn away by death, they go
>   Reluctant from their splendid feasts,
> Condemned in hottest flames to dwell,
> And find the spacious courts of hell
>   Pav'd with the skulls of Christian Priests![53]

Wesley underscores that the pastoral office is corrupt because of priests who are filled with avarice, pride, and ambition. They are more concerned with achieving positions of high rank than with aiding those in need. These priests are clad with the "pomp of office." Though they claim the church to be the center of their concern and that they are "the temple of the Lord," they abuse their legal power. Overcome with greed, they even seize that which belongs to the church. While they increase their own wealth, they plunder the house of a poor widow. Charles is convinced that this kind of behavior leads to the ultimate demise of such priests.

Charles Wesley greatly fears the corruption of wealth, for he has often read Luke 18:25, "It is easier for a camel to go through the eyes of a needle, than for a rich man to enter into the kingdom of God."

> Who wealth possesses here,[54]
> And is by wealth possessed,
> Can never in his sight appear
>   By whom the poor are blessed:
> His riches he enjoys,
>   On them for help relies,
> And loses for terrestrial toys
>   A kingdom in the skies.

A Eucharistic Life

From Charles Wesley's perspective, at the center of life and ministry with the poor is the eucharistic life. The table of the Lord is the focal point for all life. It presents the fullest expression of God's love for all humankind and mutual love for one another. It is the point of departure for all living, all ministry, and the life of the church. In *Redemption Hymns* (1747), Charles

---

53. The last line is a saying of St. John Chrysostom.

54. *Unpub. Poetry*, 2: 172, MS Luke, 267.

responds to the story of the great supper in Luke 14:16–24, in which the owner of the house revises his plans and invites the poor, maimed, halt, and blind to a great feast. He expresses very clearly in a lengthy poem an inclusive eucharistic theology and explicitly names the poor and marginalized as ones invited to commune.

1. Come, sinners, to the gospel-feast;[55]
    Let every soul be Jesu's guest.
    Ye need not one be left behind,
    For God hath bid all humankind.

2. Sent by my Lord, on you I call,
    The invitation is to all,
    Come, all the world: come, sinner, thou,
    All things in Christ are ready now.

    . . .

12. Come, then ye souls, by sin opprest,
    Ye restless wanderers after rest;
    Ye poor, and maimed, and halt, and blind,
    In Christ a hearty welcome find.

13. Sinners my gracious Lord receives,
    Harlots, and publicans, and thieves,
    Drunkards, and all the hellish crew,
    I have a message now to you.

14. Come, and partake the gospel-feast,
    Be saved from sin, in Jesus rest:
    O taste the goodness of our God,
    And eat his flesh, and drink his blood.

    . . .

17. The worst unto my supper press,
    Monsters of daring wickedness,
    Tell them, my grace for all is free,
    They cannot be too bad for me.

    . . .

55. *Redemption Hymns* (1747), 63–66, no. 50, stanzas 1–2, 12, 20, and 24; titled "The Great Supper, Luke xiv. 16–24."

24. This is the time, no more delay,
    This is the acceptable day,
    Come in, this moment, at his call,
    And live for him who died for all.

In stanza 1 of this poem is found the hallmark of radical grace and justice for the poor: "Ye need not one be left behind." Yet the church in every age need only survey those present at the Lord's table and in its worship services to determine very quickly who has been left behind. Very often it is the poor. God's invitation, however, is not to a select few or to a particular group; rather, says Wesley, "God hath bid all humankind."

Charles states clearly: "Let *every soul* be Jesu's guest . . . The invitation is to *all* / Come *all the world.*" In stanza 12, he specifically names the poor, along with the maimed, halt, and blind, among those welcome at the table. In stanza 13, he extends the list of marginalized to include harlots, publicans, thieves, and drunkards. He goes a step further in stanza 17, saying that "monsters of daring wickedness" are also invited. All of those enumerated by Wesley in this lengthy hymn would not have been the most likely people invited to the Lord's table in a parish church of eighteenth-century England. Nevertheless, he emphasized that they are unequivocally invited. God's radical grace invites all to the table.

In stanzas 17 and 24, Charles emphasizes the heart of Wesleyan theology: God's "grace for *all* is free" and Christ's followers are to "live for him who died for *all.*" Every minister of the gospel, indeed every Christian, has the mandate to declare: "The invitation is to all. / Come, all the world!" This holy meal to which all are invited is the place where hearts are constrained or fully captivated by love, God's love.

In "An Elegy on the Death of Robert Jones, Esq. of Fonmon-Castle, in Glamorganshire, South Wales," Charles remembers a gentleman who understood the centrality of the eucharistic life enlivened by outreach to the poor and marginalized.

230 No voice was heard, but that of prayer and praise.[56]

    Divinely taught to make the sober feast,
    He passed the rich, and called a nobler guest;
    He called the poor, the maimed, the lame, the blind,
    He called in these the Saviour of mankind;

---

56. Charles Wesley, *Elegy on the Death of Robert Jones, Esq. of Fonmon Castle in Glamorganshire, South Wales*, 12–13. Line numbers are given to the left.

235 His friends and kinsmen these for Jesu's sake,
　　Who no voluptuous recompence could make,
　　But God the glorious recompence hath given,
　　And called him to the marriage-feast in heaven.

　　. . .

258 After the Lamb he still rejoiced to go,
　　He lived a guardian angel here below,
　　A father to the poor, he gave them food,
　　And fed their souls, and laboured for their good.

Jones was "Divinely taught to make the sober feast," and in the spirit of the great supper of Matthew 14, he invited "the poor, the maimed, the lame, the blind." He did not invite them merely out of generosity and kindness; in inviting them, he invited the Savior of all: "He called in these the Saviour of mankind." Clearly Christ's identity with the poor was apparent to Jones. Furthermore, he calls them his "friends and kinsmen." He knew all too well that they could not reciprocate; they could make no recompense for the invitation. That was not what he sought.

No doubt Charles is lifting up the life of Mr. Jones as an example of how to live so that there is justice for the poor. "He lived a guardian angel here below." He was a "father to the poor." Not only did he feed their bodies and souls, he "laboured for their good." It is perhaps very easy to feed the poor, but to be a father to them means that one enters a familial and intimate relationship. Furthermore, Jones worked for the good of the poor. In other words, he invested time and effort on their behalf for the betterment of their lives. All of this flowed from the center of the "sober feast," the eucharistic life. This is where justice for the poor begins, for there one discovers the fullness of self-giving love for all people.

DISCIPLESHIP

While Charles Wesley passionately preached the gospel to the poor, he was just as passionate about meeting their physical and earthly needs. This was an integral part of his witness among the poor that required action instead of words.

How does one live a life of service to the poor? How can one be a faithful disciple in this regard? Perhaps there are no simple answers to these questions. Charles, however, is very specific about faithful Christian behavior with and among the poor and marginalized.

Service to the Poor

Charles Wesley's lifelong desire to serve the poor is expressed in the following couplet:

O might I thus thro' life endure,[57]
Serve my Saviour in the poor.

I have often called stanza 2 of another poem that remained unpublished at his death the "Social Manifesto" of the Wesleyan movement. It is a response to Acts 20:35, "I have showed you all things, how that so labouring ye ought to support the weak, and to remember the words of the Lord Jesus, how he said, It is more blessed to give than to receive."

1. Your duty let th' Apostle show;[58]
    Ye ought, ye ought to labour so,
        In Jesus' cause employed,
    Your calling's works at times pursue,
    And keep the Tentmaker[59] in view,
        And use your hands for God.

2. Work for the weak, and sick, and poor,
    Raiment and food for them procure,
        And mindful of his word,
    Enjoy the blessedness to give,
    Lay out your gettings to relieve
        The members of your Lord.

3. Your labour, which proceeds from love,
    Jesus shall graciously approve,
        With full felicity,
    With brightest crowns your loan repay,
    And tell you in that joyful day,
        "Ye did it unto me."

Stanza 3 provides two foci as the starting points for all outreach to the poor and marginalized: (1) It "proceeds from love." Indeed, for Charles Wesley, "love" is the key to all ethical understanding and human behavior. (2) Service to the "the weak, and sick, and poor" is service to Christ: "You did it unto me."

57. *Unpub. Poetry,* 2:69, MS Mark, 182.
58. Ibid., 2:403–4, MS Acts 420.
59. The Apostle Paul.

Note that in stanza 1 Charles does speak of "an option" of service to those in need. He repeats: "ye *ought*, ye *ought* to labor so." This is what followers of Christ should be doing! When you are working for the good of others you are employed in the cause of Christ. Wesley then paints an interesting mental image: "keep the tentmaker [St. Paul] in view, / and use your hands for God." Do not be afraid of manual labor, especially for those in need.

In stanza 2, "The Social Manifesto," Charles becomes programmatic. Christians are admonished to "Work for the weak, and sick, and poor." He qualifies what it means to work for them: one is to lay out one's earnings on their behalf, and one is to procure "raiment and food for them." This means that whatever one does professionally or vocationally should generate income that fosters aid for the less fortunate. This is not an ethical option, but a mandate based upon the scriptural commission of Acts 20. Hence, it is no coincidence that Wesley says in stanza 2 to be "mindful of God's word." It is the authority from which his ethical posture emerges throughout his entire life.

Often Charles acknowledged in his poetry those who exemplified the ethical posture of service to the poor. In the sixth and seventh stanzas of a tribute titled "On the Death of Mr. Thomas Lewis, who Died at Bristol, [April] 1782," he wrote:

> His heart, as tender as sincere,[60]
> Melted for ev'ry sufferer,
>   And bled for the distressed,
> Whene'er he heard the grieved complain;
> And pity for the sons of pain,
>   Resided in his breast.
>
> A father to the sick and poor,
> For them he husbanded his store,
>   For them himself denied;
> The naked clothed, the hungry fed,
> Or parted with his daily bread
>   That they might be supplied.

The familial language of "father to the sick and poor" indicates, as we have seen earlier, a close relationship with those in need. Charles also stresses

---

60. *Arminian Magazine* 6 (1783) 50, stanzas 6 and 7 (of a twelve-stanza poem); Jackson, *Journal*, 2:406.

self-denial in serving the less fortunate. In appropriating his own resources, Thomas Lewis denied himself that others might be clothed and fed. He willingly did without his own daily food in order that others might not go hungry.

These poetical lines are meant to inspire others to live as Lewis lived.

> O! That the friends he leaves beneath,[61]
> Might live his life, and die his death,
>> For glory as mature,
> Partakers with the saints in light,
> And read the pleasures in thy sight,
>> Which ever more endure!

If you want to know how to live, Wesley says, "live his life, and die his death." If you do, you will be a parent to the sick and poor. You will use your resources to clothe the naked and feed the hungry.

Charles Wesley cautions the community of faith that failing to reach out to serve the poor is a failure to follow the admonition of Scripture and to meet human need. The following poem was precipitated by reading James 2:15–16: "If a brother be naked and destitute of daily food, and one of you say unto them, Depart in peace, be ye warmed and filled; notwithstanding ye give them not those things which are needful to the body; what doth it profit?"

> What doth thy Gnostick faith avail,[62]
>> Who seest thy brother in distress,
> With ruthless heart insensible,
>> And bidst the poor depart in peace,
> Yet dost not his distress relieve,
> But words without assistance give!

What does it benefit anyone, to know that there are people in need and in distress, to stand in their presence, and yet to send them on their way, doing nothing to aid them? Charles says this is evidence of a ruthless, insensible heart! Can he possibly be speaking of Christians when he mentions those of "Gnostick faith"?

61. Ibid., 51, stanza 12.
62. *Scripture Hymns* (1762), 2:381, Hymn no. 743.

Stewardship of Resources

Charles Wesley was concerned that there be a deep sense of committed stewardship among the disciples of Christ. The following verses from Acts 4 inspired one of the few stewardship hymns he penned: "Neither was there any among them that lacked: for as many as were possessors of lands or houses sold them, and brought the prices of the things that were sold, and laid them down at the apostles' feet: and distribution was made unto each as any had need" (34–35). Reflecting on these words, Charles wrote:

1.   Which of the Christians now[63]
    Would their possessions sell?
The fact you scarce allow,
    The truth incredible:
That saints of old so weak should prove
And as themselves their neighbour love.

2.   Of your abundant[64] store
    You may a few relieve,
But all to feed the poor
    You cannot, cannot give,
Houses and lands for Christ forego,
Or live as Jesus lived below.

3.   Jesus, thy church inspire
    With apostolic love,
Infuse the one desire
    T' insure our wealth above,
Freely with earthly goods to part,
And joyfully sell all in heart.

4.   With thy pure Spirit filled,
    And loving thee alone,
We shall our substance yield,
    Call nothing here our own,
Whate'er we have or are submit
And lie, as beggars, at thy feet.

63. *Unpub. Poetry*, 2:297–98, MS Acts, 74–75.

64. Charles originally wrote "redundant" and then struck through that word and wrote "abundant."

What a penetrating question: Who among the Christians is willing to sell their possessions? Wesley says that this is a possibility that few would even consider. Then, in a very sarcastic tone, he says—imagine this—there were actually some saints of long ago (as the Acts passage reveals) who were *so weak* that they loved their neighbors as themselves. Even if this seems impossible to consider, there were some people, according to the biblical text, who sold their possessions and gave all the proceeds for the good of anyone in need.

Perhaps in stanza 2 Charles is speaking as a husband and father when he says that you cannot give *all* to feed the poor or live as Jesus did. Nevertheless, in stanza 3 he prays for the inspiration of apostolic love, the kind of love that inspired the faithful in Acts 4 to give so freely. The Christian must be willing to part with earthly goods.

The key to Charles's understanding of Christian stewardship is found in stanza 4. If we are filled with God's Spirit and love God alone, we will be willing to call nothing on earth our own. We submit all that we are and have to God, the source of all things. We may even give out of our poverty, as Charles emphasizes in a brief poem about the widow's gift of two coins recorded in Luke 21, particularly verse 4: "But she of her poverty hath cast in all the living that she had."

> God his mighty power displays,[65]
>   God his love to sinners shows;
> Free, and disengaged by grace
>   Then the poor his all bestows;
> Let his whole provision fail,
>   She his confidence approves,
> Feasts a Friend invisible,
>   One whom more than life he loves.

In another poem that remained unpublished at his death, Charles Wesley discusses the sharing of one's resources with others in the context of a spirit of unity and mutual concern. The poem is a response to Acts 4:32, "The multitude of them that believed, were of one heart, and one soul; neither said any of them, that aught of the things which he possessed, was his own, but they had all things in common. Neither was there any among them that lacked."

---

65. *Unpub. Poetry,* 2:187.

1. Happy the multitude[66]
       (But far above our sphere)
    Redeemed by Jesus' blood
       From all we covet here!
    To him, and to each other joined,
       They all were of one heart and mind.

2. His blood the cement was
       Who died on Calvary,
    And fastened to his cross
       They could not disagree:
    One soul did all the members move,
    The soul of harmony and love.

3. Their goods were free to all,
       Appropriated to none,
    While none presumed to call
       What he possessed his own;
    The diff'rence base of *thine* and *mine*
    Was lost in charity Divine.

4. No overplus, no need,
       No rich or poor were there,
    Content with daily bread
       Where all enjoyed their share;
    With every common blessing blessed
    They nothing had, yet all possessed.

This poem is an extremely strong statement of radical grace. Charles paints a picture of the church in which possessions do not create divisions. Is this picture simply idealistic and unrealistic for the church of the eighteenth century and of any age? The multitude of people is joined to Christ and to one another. They are of "one heart and mind." One thing moves the members of Christ's body, the church, namely, the soul of harmony and love.

Many would consider stanza 3 as unachievable and contrary to capitalism and self-determination, for it says that "Their goods were free for all, / Appropriated to none." No one presumed to call anything a personal possession. Then comes a striking averment—the words "*thine* and *mine*" disappear from the vocabulary of the followers of Christ, for everything is lost in divine love to which all creation owes everything.

66. *Unpub. Poetry*, 2:295–96, MS Acts, 71–72.

Finally, Wesley describes the ideal of the community of faith. Yes, he is describing the communal experience of Acts 4, but he is also holding up this ideal to the church of the eighteenth century and all future ages. There is no excess and no need! The societal categories of rich and poor are obliterated, and all are to share commonly! This is the ultimate result of radical grace. Imagine—"They nothing had, yet all possessed." Why? They had discovered "the soul of harmony and love" in Jesus Christ.

While Charles emphasizes time and again the importance of sharing one's resources with the less fortunate, he also stresses that almsgiving itself does not suffice for the life committed to Christ and the church. Furthermore, one does not gain the pleasure of God by giving to others. Indeed, God has commanded all who would be faithful to help the poor. However, if we have truly left our sins behind, it will be our natural posture to aid those in need.

In responding to Luke 3:11, "He that hath two coats let him impart to him that hath none," Charles writes:

> Alms cannot alone, we know,[67]
>   Cannot grace from God procure,
> Yet at his command we show
>   Mercy to the helpless poor;
> When our sins we truly leave,
>   We our neighbour's wants supply,
> Till to us the Saviour give
>   Food and raiment from the sky.

Friendship with the Poor

We have already encountered the passage in Charles's *MSJ* in which he calls the poor his best friends. It is not surprising that he wrote three poems that use the word *friend* in relation to the poor. Only one of them was published during his lifetime. In the first, he sees the poor as Jesus' closest friends, or "bosom-friends," which motivates his followers to make the poor their "dearest care." The hitherto unpublished poem is based on Acts 20:35–36: "I have showed you all things, how that so labouring ye ought to support the weak, and to remember the words of the Lord Jesus, how he said, it is more blessed to give than to receive. And when he had thus spoken, he kneeled down, and prayed with them all."

67. *Unpub. Poetry*, 2:87, MS Luke, 43.

The poor as Jesus' bosom-friends,[68]
    The poor he makes his latest care,
To all his successors commends,
    And wills us on our hands to bear;
The poor our dearest care we make,
    Aspiring to superior bliss,
And cherish for their Saviour's sake,
    And love them with a love like his.

If the poor are Jesus' "bosom-friends," they are extremely intimate friends. He makes them "his latest care." His is not a casual concern for the poor; rather, he is deeply concerned for them. According to Charles, Jesus entrusts this same caring concern to his followers. It is his will that the poor be cared for.

In line 5, Wesley shifts from the third person descriptive narrative about Jesus and the poor to the first person plural and how Jesus' followers are to respond to his example. "The poor our dearest care we make." There can be no misunderstanding what he is saying here. The members of the church of Jesus Christ must have an enduring central focus on ministry to the poor and marginalized. They will cherish them for his sake, and they will love the poor with a love like that of Christ. Wesley's ideas in this poem are not mere conjecture; they come directly from the biblical passage on which it is based.

The second poem, which follows a similar emphasis, was published in *Hymns of Intercession for All Mankind* (1758) and is titled "For the Fatherless Children."

Relieve whoe'er thy succour need,[69]
    A Father to the orphans be,
Who dost the hungry ravens feed,
    Provide for all that cry to thee,
The poor and fatherless defend,
    Their sure, their everlasting friend.

While Jesus is often spoken of as the everlasting Friend, here Charles Wesley specifically applies this term to the followers of Jesus who, in aiding the poor and fatherless, become "Their sure, their everlasting friend."

The third poem, which remained unpublished at Wesley's death, is based on Luke 16:9: "Make to yourselves friends of the mammon of

---

68. Poem 1: *Unpub. Poetry,* 2:404, MS Acts, 421.

69. Poem 2: *Hymns of Intercession,* (1758) no. 28, 24.

unrighteousness; that, when ye fail, they may receive you into everlasting habitations."

> Whate'er thou dost to us entrust,[70]
>   With thy peculiar blessing blessed,
> O make us diligent and just,
>   As stewards faithful to the least,
> Endowed with wisdom to possess
> The mammon of unrighteousness.
>
> Help us to make the poor our friends,
>   By that which paves the way to hell,
> That when our loving labour ends,
>   And dying from this earth we fail,
> Our friends may greet us in the skies
> Born to a life that never dies.

At first glance, it may seem difficult to grasp the intent of Charles's prayer in this poem. What can he mean by asserting that Christ's followers, as Luke's Gospel says, should make themselves "friends of the mammon of unrighteousness"? The answer comes in the second stanza, in which he makes clear that the "mammon of unrighteousness"—money—is to be used for a righteous purpose: to make friends of the poor. Christians are to make the poor their friends by sharing their resources with them. Rather than paving the way to hell, their resources will pave the way to heaven, where those who have been befriended will "greet us in the skies."

Mutual Assistance

Charles Wesley understands Christian community in the light of the New Testament to be one of mutual support for one another. This is not a question of encouraging dependency of some on others, but rather of persons joined in fellowship. Wesley wrote a lengthy poetical prayer on this subject that was published in 1742. Stanzas pertinent to this discussion are as follows:

> A Prayer for Persons Joined in Fellowship
>   Jesu, united by thy grace[71]
>   And each to each endeared,
>   With confidence we seek thy face
>   And know our prayer is heard.

70. Poem 3: *Unpub. Poetry*, 2:157, MS Luke, 232–33.
71. *HSP* (1742), original Part IV: 1, 86.

Help us to help each other, Lord,[72]
  Each other's cross to bear,
Let all their friendly aid afford,
  And feel each other's[73] care.

Help us to build each other up,
  Our little stock improve;
Increase our faith, confirm our hope,
  And perfect us in love.

Touched by the lodestone of thy love,[74]
  Let all our hearts agree,
And ever towards each other move,
  And ever move towards thee.

Here Charles prays for a community of faith in which each person is endeared to the other. This, too, is a radical view, for where are the churches, throughout history and in the present day, in which every person has shown such mutual affection? Such radical grace is truly lived only when there is mutual endearment. As cynical as it may sound to say that the church has never achieved such a state, Wesley is not without hope that God can make it possible. Hence, he prays: "With confidence we seek thy face, / And know our prayer is heard."

Wesley continues to pray for God's assistance in the next stanza ("Help us to help each other, Lord"), for he knows that human beings do not always help one another. Their tendency is to help themselves first. He plumbs the depth of the human psyche when he prays for enablement to bear someone else's cross. Is bearing one's own cross not enough? Must we bear someone else's as well? Wesley believes we must. How is this possible? It is more than just taking up someone else's problems and aiding in their solution. One must lend friendly aid! Yes, but more—one must "feel" the other's care. How is this possible? It involves all of the things Wesley experienced in his relationships with the poor: conversation, prayer, shared worship and fellowship at the Lord's table, friendship, sharing the gospel, love, and resources. Only in these ways can we "feel" another's care.

The third stanza stresses the importance of mutual support for one another. Wesley prays: "Help us to build each other up." One wonders what the church of Jesus Christ might have been like through the ages, if

72. Ibid., stanzas 2–3 are original Part 1: 2–4, 83.
73. Original: "each brother's" and previous line original: "his friendly aid."
74. Ibid., original Part IV: 4, 86.

it had sought to make such a prayer a reality. Of course, there have been some organized efforts to seek mutual cooperation of denominations, but when one thinks of the plethora of Christian churches throughout the world, the multiplicity of para-church groups, and other organizations that support themselves first (even when they profess as their sole purpose the proclamation of the Christian gospel and the living of a Christian ethic), one must ask: To what extent do they really seek to build each other up? We must not forget the poor here, for as Wesley reminds us, the kingdom of God is revealed in and through them. Therefore, if we are praying to build up each other, we are also including the poor. As we seek to build up each other, our faith will be increased and our hope confirmed, and we shall move toward perfection in love.

The final stanza stresses that if we are touched by the magnetism of God's love in Christ, our hearts will be as one. The love of Christ works like a magnet and draws people together as one. When Charles prays in the last stanza above for the agreement of hearts, he is not praying for agreement in all matters of intellect. Even if there is not agreement in all matters of the mind, there can be agreement in matters of the heart. The unity of hearts is far more important, for it motivates people to move toward each other, including the poor and marginalized, and to move toward God.

Oppose War and Advocate Peace

Charles Wesley's views on war and peace are vitally important in a discussion on justice for the poor and marginalized, because in times of war it is often the poor and dispossessed who suffer the most, especially women and children. Without peace there can be no justice. One cannot be a committed Christian and refuse to ask oneself, "What is my attitude toward war? The killing of other human beings? Can war be just?"

Have we taught our children the Gospel lesson of Luke 10:5, "Into whatsoever house you enter, first say, Peace"? What a message for times of peace and war! Do we dare say, "Peace" when we enter the homes of friends and enemies? Do war colleges have multilingual lexicons with words for peace? What a haunting thought—that soldiers would have on their lips, as the first word upon entering the home of "the enemy," *peace, salaam, shalom, paix, friede, pax, pas.* Indeed, this would be an act of radical grace.

Charles Wesley reflected on these words from Luke's Gospel and wrote the following poignant lines.

1. Peace to this house! The greatest good[75]
   Which sinners can from God receive!
   The peace Divine on all bestowed
   Who in a proffered Christ believe,
   The peace which seals your sins forgiven,
   And brings you here a taste of heaven.

2. We cannot wish our neighbour more
   Than present and eternal peace,
   The riches these of Jesus' poor,
   With which the sons of men we bless,
   And spread through earth the precious prize,
   And turn it into paradise.

Present peace and eternal peace, says Charles, are the riches of Jesus' poor, and these riches are to bless "the sons of men," meaning "all humankind." The peace of Jesus' poor is the source of worldwide blessing. Are we prepared to "spread through earth the precious prize" of peace "and turn [earth] into paradise," as he suggests? This is radical grace in action.

Do Charles Wesley's views help followers of Christ in the current context of wars raging around the world? Some Christians are avowed pacifists, many oppose war but are not necessarily pacifists, others passionately support war, while still others are victims of war.

In the struggle to shape our attitudes about war and peace, we may turn to Wesley for wisdom. While he lived in the eighteenth century, was loyal to the British monarchy, and was not an avowed pacifist, he was a ardent opponent of war. We learn this immediately from his response to Isaiah 2:4, "Neither shall they learn war any more."

1.   Messias, Prince of peace,[76]
   Where men each other tear,
   Where war is learnt, they must confess
   Thy kingdom is not there:

---

75. MS Luke, 147; see *Poet. Works* 11:191, no. 1346.

76. *Scripture Hymns* (1762), 1:305, no. 960.

Who prompted by thy foe
Delight in human blood,
Apollyon is their king, they show,
And Satan is their god.

2.   But shall he still devour
The souls redeemed by thee?
Jesus, stir up thy glorious power,
And end th' apostasy;
Come, Saviour, from above
O'er all the earth to reign,
And plant the kingdom of thy love
In every heart of man.

3.   Then shall we exercise
The hellish art no more,
While thou our long-lost paradise
Dost with thyself restore;
Fightings and wars shall cease,
And in thy Spirit given
Pure joy, and everlasting peace
Shall turn our earth to heaven.

In this poem from *Scripture Hymns* (1762), Wesley prays for the day when there shall be no more war. He is not longing merely for some distant paradise, however, for in stanza 2 he prays for love to be planted in every human heart at this very moment. Wesley is clear: where there is war, there is no reign of God ("Your kingdom is not there"). Once again Charles espouses a radical view.

He is not content to wait passively for God to do everything to bring the advent of peace. If the seeds of love are planted in human hearts, they must be nurtured to mature growth. Wesley is confident with the prophet Isaiah that it is possible to *unlearn* war. "Neither shall they *learn* war any more." To unlearn war is an act of radical grace.

Christ's followers, says Wesley, are those who do not wish to exercise the "hellish art of war"; rather, they wish to "end th' apostasy" of war, to "turn our earth to heaven," and to end "fightings and wars." They are advocates of the loving peace Christ incarnates and brings to reign on earth. They are advocates of such radical grace.

Having read Isaiah 11:9, Charles Wesley prays for the end of war:

Lord of hosts, thy power assume,[77]
　　Thy sway thro' earth extend,
Then destructive war shall come
　　To a perpetual end.

How is God's "sway thro' earth" extended? By God's followers implementing the divine opposition to destructive war. The reign of God's love in human hearts is the only way that war can be brought to a "perpetual end." This is what Christ brings! He brings the radical grace with which the Christmas hymn "Hark! the herald angels sing" resounds:

Peace on earth and mercy mild,[78]
God and sinners reconciled.

This is not only the song of the angels; rather, it is the song of *all* Christians, who should spend their lives singing and living the message of this song! The Christ we follow brings peace.

　　In a hymn for Pentecost titled "For the Fruits of the Spirit," Wesley pleads:

1. Jesus, God of peace and love,[79]
　Send thy blessing from above,
　Take, and seal us for thine own,
　Touch our hearts, and make us one.

2. By the sense of sin forgiven
　Purge out all the former leaven:
　Malice, guile, and proud offence;
　Take the stone of stumbling hence.

3. Root up every bitter root,
　Multiply the Spirit's fruit:
　Love, and joy, and quiet peace,
　Meek long-suffering, gentleness.

4. Strict and general temperance
　Boundless pure benevolence,
　Cordial, firm fidelity,
　All the mind which was in thee.

77. *Scripture Hymns* (1762), 1:317, no. 991.

78. *HSP* (1739), 206.

79. *Whitsunday Hymns*, 28–29, Hymn 25. The hymn may be sung to the tune "Messiah" (*UMH* 399).

Wesley yearns for all humankind to be united in God's peace and love. He prays that malice, guile, proud offense, and the bitter root will be removed from us so that Jesus' mind may dwell within us. These are to be replaced by love, joy, quiet peace, meek long-suffering, and gentleness. We have yet to encounter a society filled with "boundless pure benevolence" and "cordial, firm fidelity," but these are the qualities that emerge when we are captivated by God's peace and love.

Charles Wesley published the hymn "Our earth we now lament to see" in *Hymns of Intercession for All Mankind* (1758) with the title "For Peace." When his brother John published it in *A Collection of Hymns for the Use of the People Called Methodists* (1780), it was included in the section titled "For Believers Interceding for the World." It is included in *The United Methodist Hymnal* at number 449, where it appears without music. It should be read over and over in private and public worship, however, and congregations should learn to sing it, perhaps to the well-known tune "St. Catherine," number 710 in *The United Methodist Hymnal* (and found in many other hymnals).

The hymn, composed in a century riddled with war and rumors of war, may reflect public accounts of fierce battles—for example, the Battle of Culloden that took place in April 1745. It is as relevant now as it was then. Wesley uses some images that are less familiar to us today but are descriptive of the horrors of war and death. The second stanza includes satanic images from the depths of Sheol, drawn from Revelation 9:11: "They have as king over them the angel of the bottomless pit," whose name in Hebrew is Abaddon [Destruction], and in Greek Apollyon [Destroyer]. The most gruesome of religious aberrations was the sacrifice of children as burnt offerings to the god Baal at an illicit place of worship in the Valley of Hinnom, known as Tophet (2 Kgs 23:10; Lev 18:21).

Here is Charles Wesley's summons to peace and plea for the obliteration of war.

> Our earth we now lament to see[80]
>> With floods of wickedness o'erflowed,
> With violence, wrong, and cruelty,
>> One wide-extended field of blood,
> Where mortal fiends each other tear
> In all the hellish rage of war.

---

80. *Hymns of Intercession*, 4, Hymn no. II.

As listed on Abaddon's side,
    They mangle their own flesh, and slay;
Tophet is moved, and opens wide
    Its mouth for its enormous prey;
And myriads sink beneath the grave,
And plunge into the flaming wave.

O might the universal Friend
    This havoc of his creatures see!
Bid our unnatural discord end,
    Declare us reconciled in thee!
Write kindness on our inward parts
And chase the murderer from our hearts!

Who now against each other rise,
    The nations of the earth constrain
To follow after peace, and prize
    The blessings of thy righteous reign,
The joys of unity to prove,
The paradise of perfect love!

This is a Wesleyan prayer for the advent of the reign of peace, which Christ brought to earth but which has yet to be realized. If the nations of the earth are to be constrained to seek peace and justice, then it is the citizens of the nations who must be the advocates of peace. Hence, Wesley reminds us that wherever we find ourselves, we are to "follow after peace" and "prove the joys of unity." The result is "the paradise of perfect love," the fulfillment of radical grace.

    In another prayer, Charles Wesley pleads for deliverance from wars and conflicts. It is based on part of the Lucan version of the Lord's Prayer, Luke 11:4: "But deliver us from evil."

Deliver us from evil, Lord,[81]
    Thy church so dearly bought,
From every evil work, and word,
    And every evil thought:
Preserve us from the tempting fiend,
    The world of wickedness,

---

81. *Scripture Hymns* (1762), 2:222, Hymn no. 349.

'Till all our wars and conflicts end
In everlasting peace.

Finally, we turn to a lengthier prayer inspired by Isaiah 11:6–7, one of the premier passages from the Hebrew Scriptures that speaks of a just world of peace: "The wolf shall dwell with the lamb, and the leopard shall lie down with the kid: and the calf, and the young lion, and the fatling together, and a little child shall lead them. And the cow and the bear shall feed; their young ones shall lie down together: and the lion shall eat straw like the ox."

1. Prince of universal peace,[82]
   Destroy the enmity,
   Bid our jars[83] and discords cease,
   Unite us all in thee:
   Cruel as wild beasts we are,
   'Till vanquished by thy mercy's power,
   Men, like wolves, each other tear,
   And their own flesh devour.

2. But if thou pronounce the word
   That forms our souls again,
   Love and harmony restored
   Throughout the earth shall reign
   When thy wondrous love they feel,
   The human savages are tame,
   Ravenous wolves, and leopards dwell
   And stable with the lamb.

3. Bears transform'd with oxen graze,
   Their young together feed,
   With the calf the lion plays
   Nor rends the dandled kid;
   Harshest natures reconcil'd
   With soft, and fierce with meek agree,
   Gentle, tractable, and mild
   As harmless infancy.

82. *Scripture Hymns* (1762), 1:316.
83. Meaning "unpleasantness."

4. O that now with pardon blest
        We each might each embrace,
     Quietly together rest,
        And feed upon thy grace,
     Like our sinless parents live!
   Great shepherd, make thy goodness known,
        All into thy fold receive,
           And keep forever one.

The followers of Christ need to learn to pray these prayers of Charles Wesley anew "and feed upon [God's] grace." His pleas for God's intervention against war require that we be instruments of the divine peace for which we pray; in other words, we must be the embodiment of God's radical grace, which functions contrary to the way of the world. If God writes kindness on our inward parts, we must live this reality. If God chases the murderer from our hearts, we must live this reality. It is time to live God's radical grace! Thus, we share "the riches of Jesus' poor," which are present and eternal peace.

CONCLUSION

The poetry of Charles Wesley affirms and expands his perspectives on life and ministry with and among the poor that are found in his sermons and *MSJ*. He accentuates and defines more carefully the principle of inclusive love and that the poor are God's chosen people. He sets a strong tone for the creative interaction of compassion and evangelism whereby preaching the gospel to the poor interfaces with doing good to all, even to those who are not of the household of faith. Wesley sets a high standard for the clergy and holds himself accountable to the same as one gravely in danger of robbing the poor by being satisfied with living in ease. Above all, the eucharistic life was for him the beginning and end of one's life of discipleship in service to God and others. He personalized justice for the poor by being an instrument of radical grace, by following the mandate of Scripture to care for the poor.

Charles Wesley sought to practice what he preached, namely, to be continually employed in service to the poor. This was not merely a spiritualized concept about which he preached and wrote, but one he practiced. As Gareth Lloyd notes regarding entries of the West Street Chapel Poor Fund Ledger, "Sometimes specific cases are recorded in the ledger by name, such as the four shillings given to Brother Barham for bread and the money collected for Kingswood School and for the benefit of Charles Wesley's poor, presumably individuals in whom Charles took a personal interest."[84]

---

84. "Eighteenth-Century Methodism and the London Poor," in Heitzenrater, *Poor and the People Called Methodists,* 126.

IV. The Church's Response to Radical Grace

Justice for the Poor and Marginalized

SHAPING A THEOLOGY OF RADICAL GRACE

If Charles Wesley models some aspects of social outreach for the church in every age, what are the implications for the twenty-first-century church? First and foremost, it must have the following theological focus: All humankind is interrelated as creatures of God, who loves everyone and has expressed this love in Jesus Christ. Such inclusive love opposes injustice and seeks justice for all. Radical grace is expressed through Christ's followers by seeking justice for the poor.

Wesley grew up in a world of an emerging industrial revolution with rampant unemployment, economic displacement, widespread illnesses and poor medical care, the Poor Tax, and workhouses. The sin of greed or self-accumulated wealth at the expense of others, often a cause of poverty, was readily evident in eighteenth-century English society and was addressed by Charles in his poetry. There was poverty, hunger, and slavery, all of which he opposed.

Most certainly, however, the "new poor" of the twenty-first century cannot be equated with the poor of the eighteenth century. José Míguez Bonino rightly observes: "The contemporary poor clearly represent a different poverty in a different world from Wesley's. While our poor suffer just as those of eighteenth-century Britain, ours are in a qualitatively different condition in their social prospects, expectations, and attitudes."[1]

Therefore, one asks: How can Charles Wesley's perspectives regarding the poor aid us in ministering to them today?

---

1. "The Poor Will Always Be with You," in Heitzenrater, *Poor and the People Called Methodists*, 187. See John Wesley's *Thoughts on the Scarcity of Provisions* (1773).

Charles's approach is different from that of his brother John. While Charles laments and denounces the state of the poor and commends works of mercy on their behalf, John in his writings attempts "to understand the social, economic, and political conditions that produce poverty."[2] Charles at times seems less concerned with the misdirected laws of his day and the causes of poverty than with ministering directly to those in dire need.

Where Charles and John wholeheartedly agree is in the motivation for works of mercy and serving the poor. This is not merely a moral duty, that is, the obligation of Christ's followers. Acts of charity are not obligatory. Charles says we do them freely. They are motivated by the "principle of love to God." We do them cheerfully for God's sake. One does not have to pressure Christians to serve others. As Randy Maddox maintains, "On the one hand, he [John Wesley] made it quite clear that the main reason for participating in the means of grace was not obedience to Divine command, or the human attempt to craft holy virtues, but the simple fact that we receive through them the forgiving and empowering Presence of God's grace."[3]

Charles does speak of moral duty as noted in the following poem cited earlier, which remained unpublished at his death.

1. Your duty let th' Apostle show;
   Ye ought, ye ought to labour so,
       In Jesus' cause employed,
   Your calling's works at times pursue,
   And keep the Tentmaker[4] in view,
       And use your hands for God.

2. Work for the weak, and sick, and poor,
   Raiment and food for them procure,
       And mindful of God's word,
   Enjoy the blessedness to give,
   Lay out your gettings to relieve
       The members of your Lord.

If Wesley had stopped at the end of stanza 2, one might conclude that he comes down clearly on the side of strict moral obligation. In other words, one fulfills the mandate of the Hebrew and Greek Scriptures to care for the

---

2. Heitzenrater, *Poor and the People Called Methodists*, 187.

3. *Responsible Grace*, 201.

4. The Apostle Paul.

poor, because the Scripture requires it. There is a third stanza, however, which clarifies the motivation for acts of moral responsibility.

3. Your labour, which proceeds from love,
    Jesus shall graciously approve,
        With full felicity,
    With brightest crowns your loan repay,
    And tell you in that joyful day,
        "Ye did it unto me."

Whatever we do for others issues from love with the awareness that not only are we assisting the needy, we are doing what we do for Christ.

Charles lived by the reality that there is no privileged class in God's realm. All are recipients of God's loving grace in Jesus Christ. Unfortunately, so much of the poetry he penned that addresses poverty and the poor in his day was left unpublished at his death. Therefore, we can find only a delimited response to his perspectives on justice for the poor and marginalized in his published works. Since the publication of his "complete" corpus of poetry, it is possible to see him in a larger context.[5]

Ted A. Campbell, relying heavily on Charles Wesley's hitherto unpublished verse, sees his ideas on poverty and the poor as in concert with the mendicant poor of the medieval period, particularly as relates to the following themes: the poor Christ (or poverty of Christ), the poor as Christ's beloved, and the call to voluntary poverty.[6] "Charles Wesley's verse comes much closer to the distinctiveness of mendicant understandings of the poor than John Wesley's prose."[7] In this sense, perhaps, Charles's perspectives are more pastoral. While one cannot merely transfer them to the twenty-first century, the broad contours of his views have vital implications for the church today.

Like his brother John, Charles challenges the church to be courageous and step beyond the boundaries of its walls and hierarchies in order to actualize acts of compassion and justice. Nevertheless, one cannot blindly apply his views and analyses to the poor today. Poverty today emerges in such diverse and complex ways that the comparisons across

5. See *Unpub. Poetry*, 3 vols., and the Web site of the Center for Studies in the Wesleyan Tradition of the Divinity School of Duke University, where all of Charles Wesley's published and manuscript verse may be found.

6. "The Image of Christ in the Poor," in Heitzenrater, *Poor and the People Called Methodists*, 49–54.

7. Ibid., 56.

three centuries reveal a radically different picture. Economic globalization has reshaped the world and created the "new poor." International corporations often wield more power than nations themselves, and the "holy grail" of the market often causes the demise of societal structures and educational and health options as recessions paralyze economies worldwide and national debts soar.

Unquestionably Charles Wesley indicts the accumulation of wealth, especially as a cause of poverty, and in his poetry one finds a thoughtful, ethical, and theological critique of greed as a mechanism for robbing the poor.

Charles's brother John indeed sought ways to address the inequities of society that caused poverty and enabled the poor to break free of poverty's grasp. In 1748 he set up a lending program with thirty pounds of seed money. These funds were to be used to aid small businesses. Loans of a maximum of twenty shillings per individual were made at no interest. The term of each loan was three months with the requirement of weekly payments. Within the first eighteen months of this program, over two hundred people were given a loan. Richard Heitzenrater notes that this loan program assisted "the poor, who were more often than not business people who were underemployed or going through hard times."[8] That reads very much like a twenty-first-century comment.

The dissimilarities between the twenty-first century and the eighteenth century are very great. Not only has economic globalization caused displacement of peoples and recession among nations, but there are vast regions of the world today where seemingly endless wars have ravaged the land and the people, resulting in hunger, displaced populations, rampant disease and sickness, and especially the abuse of women and children. Natural disasters—earthquakes, droughts, hurricanes, typhoons, and tsunamis—have devastated and sometimes completely wiped out cities and populations, leaving only death, hunger, sickness, and poverty in their wake. Many of the populations affected are much larger than anything the Wesleys confronted in their day.

How can the church create a memory of justice for the poor and marginalized that will not allow it to forget this vital aspect of Christian living and will spur it to wed compassion and evangelism with decisive action?

At the New Room in Bristol, the first meetinghouse of early Methodism in England's West Country, every person entering and exiting was reminded of the importance of helping the poor. On the main door

8. Ibid., Appendix 3, Section "35. Methodist Lending Program," 233.

there was an inscribed metal plate, which is still there, with a slot for alms, and on the other side of the door there was a corresponding inscribed metal plate. They were clearly placed there to encourage people gathering for worship to give to the poor before they entered or as they departed. On the plates are etched the following Bible verses:

> Give to the poor & thou shalt have treasure in heaven. Mk. 10.21
> He that hath mercy on the poor, happy is he. Prov. 14:21

On the lower righthand corner of each plate is the year: 1755.

The irony of this powerful visual image for worshipers coming to the New Room in Bristol today is that the metal plates are so blackened and tarnished that one can no longer read what is inscribed on them unless one gets very, very close, with a bright light over one's shoulder or in one's hand. I was able to distinguish all the words only by taking a piece of paper and a pencil and making a "rubbing," as one does on a gravestone.

Is this picture of inscribed doorplates that are almost illegible a commentary on the contemporary church? That is, has the concern for the poor become so tarnished that the faithful are no longer aware of the scriptural mandate to give to the poor and to show them compassion? The time has come to polish the inscription and renew this vital image of the Wesleyan heritage—to place before the community of faith visual reminders of the responsibility to give to the poor and to show them compassion. All who enter and leave places of worship should see before them reminders of the scriptural admonition to care for the poor. Today there are, of course, numerous multimedia options that can generate images to awaken the awareness of worshippers of their responsibility to the poor.

How can Charles Wesley possibly aid us in addressing today's poor and marginalized? As we draw on the experience and thought of Charles Wesley, let us consider the following aspects shaping a theology of radical grace in the church today. This chapter concludes with suggestions for the implementation of such a theology based on principles Charles delineated in his writings and ministry.

Constant Employment

In his sermon on Titus 3:8, Charles says, "Let it be your constant employment to serve and relieve your Saviour in his poor distressed members." What does this mean for the contemporary church? It requires taking risks, which the church is often reluctant to do. This does not mean that serving the poor is the *subtext* of all that the church members do, but that it is their *constant, primary,* and *enduring concern.* In other words, Christians develop a lifestyle of commitment to the poor. In everything they do, in the way they live, the welfare of the poor should be at the heart of their concerns and activities. For many churches this means a radical transformation of annual budgets and programs.

Does one dare risk turning the stewardship programs of the church upside down? Radical grace mandates radical stewardship. Theodore W. Jennings Jr. suggests that "stewardship for the poor means that everything beyond what is necessary for life belongs to the poor."[9] Is this a viewpoint that would be endorsed by church officials and laity? How willing are clergy to exemplify such stewardship? Charles Wesley speaks of pastors who "greedily [their] pay receive" and "in splendid ease and pleasure live / by pillaging the poor." One may turn his declarative exclamation into a question: "Who dares of all vain self divest / The needy to supply"? These prophetic eighteenth-century words still ring true in the twenty-first century.

Within a capitalistic system, the plea for the redistribution of wealth is often criticized as advocating socialism or communism without considering the mandates of Scripture, the example of Jesus, and the risk of implementing radical grace. The critique of wealth and privilege brings one into conflict with the powerful sectors of society. Who will take such a risk?

It is important to emphasize, however, that Charles Wesley, as a husband and father, knew that one's family responsibilities are a definite priority. This is perhaps why he writes: "Of your abundant store / You may a few relieve, / But *all*[10] to feed the poor / You cannot, cannot give." You must care for your family. Even so, this does not relieve one of constant employment for those in need. Balancing one's own needs, the needs of one's family, and the needs of others is indeed a difficult task. Charles Wesley makes clear that the key to finding the right balance is to do whatever we do as an offering to Christ. Only in this way can the right balance be discovered.

Acquiring Virtues

Richard P. Heitzenrater has stressed that John Wesley emphasized that one may acquire virtues by the exercise of them.[11] "Thus, visiting the poor sick

9. Meeks, *Portion of the Poor,* 23.

10. Italics added.

11. Meeks, *Portion of the Poor,* 52.

is not only a sign of virtue, but also a means of acquiring virtue."[12] Charles Wesley certainly shared John's view in this matter. In all of the activities in which he was engaged with and among the poor, Charles indeed felt it was his duty to converse, worship, pray, preach the gospel, and share in Holy Communion with them. As has been emphasized a number of times previously, however, all of these acts issue from love of God and neighbor.

How does one become a friend of the poor? By befriending them. One practices friendship and thereby learns to be friendly. How does one become hospitable toward the poor? By inviting them into one's home and to one's table for a meal. Some years ago, I was somewhat surprised at what I saw when I walked into the nave of St. James Church in Bristol, England. Lining the central aisle from the back to the chancel in the front of the church were cots with mattresses and blankets. I was curious about their purpose. St. James Church had been an Anglican Church, but by the 1980s was no longer in use. In 1996, the religious order Little Brothers of Nazareth was allowed to reestablish St. James as a Roman Catholic Church. They then began the St. James Priory Project, which seeks to serve the homeless and those with substance abuse dependency. I learned that the cots were there as places for the homeless to sleep. If one visits the Web site of the St. James Priory,[13] one reads immediately its purpose and mission: "Healing, heritage, and hospitality in the heart of Bristol."

Just a few blocks from the New Room, the project's three goals of healing, heritage, and hospitality, could well be a trilogy of Wesleyan practical divinity.

> **Healing**: Our residential support and treatment for people with a substance dependency is open to all in need, whatever their background or circumstance.
>
> **Heritage**: The former Benedictine Priory of St James is the oldest building in Bristol! It has a fascinating history to tell and has witnessed almost a millennium of Bristol's development.
>
> **Hospitality**: Like our Benedictine predecessors we extend a warm welcome to all who visit. Our refectory café serves delicious refreshments and our well-equipped meeting rooms and central locality makes us an ideal venue for conferences and community group bookings.

12. Ibid.

13. http://www.stjamesprioryproject.org.uk.

St James is still a place of Christian worship and devotion but is open to all people from any faith or none.[14]

This is a contemporary realization of the spirit of the gospel of Christ that admonishes all to serve the poor and marginalized. The church building and the Little Brothers of Nazareth daily exemplify the hospitality of Christ. This is the spirit the Wesleys sought to capture in the Methodist Societies and meetinghouses. One becomes hospitable by practicing the hospitality of Christ.

How does one become a just steward of one's resources? By practicing self-denial and sharing with the poor. How does one become a humble person? By visiting and conversing with the poor, the sick, and the needy. Charles understood this superbly when he wrote:

> The poor supply thy place,
>   Deputed, Lord, by thee,
> To exercise our grace,
>   Our faith and charity,
> And what to thee in them is given,
> Is laid up for ourselves in heaven.

The poor exercise our grace, faith, and charity, and through their exercise, diverse virtues become a part of who we are—and often we are not aware that this has transpired.

Using Divine Grace

This phrase certainly sounds questionable. Is it not presumptuous to suggest that we can "use" divine grace? In a slightly different form, this idea appears as the opening line of Charles Wesley's "Covenant Hymn": "Come, let us use the grace divine."[15] God may be the author of grace, but we are the respondents to divine grace. Randy Maddox speaks of the "co-operant character" of sacramental grace.[16] Christ's followers become the implementers of the work of grace as God makes them aware of grace in diverse places and times. Thus Charles invites everyone to "use the grace divine." He foresees this act as a personal and communal one. He continues in stanza 1: "And all with one accord, / In a perpetual covenant join / Ourselves to Christ the Lord." The covenant into which *all* enter with God

14. Quoted from the St. James Priory Web site.

15. *Scripture Hymns* (1762), 2:36–37.

16. *Responsible Grace*, 196.

is always to be kept in mind: do not forsake God, do not violate his word, and forever worship the God who hears the vow we make.

The covenant made with God underscores the "co-operant character" of grace. We are responding to God's loving grace in Jesus Christ. We join ourselves to Christ the Lord. The social implications of the covenant relationship are clear when we think of the two-dimensional service paradigm: in serving others we serve God. If we promise to live and die for God, as Wesley suggests we do in the hymn, this commitment will carry over into our living for others as well, including the poor.

Wesley captures the two-dimensional service paradigm eloquently in the following lines:

> Who before the Saviour lies[17]
>   Should the mourner's task repeat;
> Penitents can never rise,
>   Never cease to kiss his feet:
> Thus may I my faith approve,
>   Lower sinking still and lower,
> Jesus in his members love,
>   Honour Jesus in the poor.

How do we use divine grace? By loving and serving the members of Christ's body, the poor. Thus we honor him!

Creating Memory

The Wesleys found in congregational song an avenue of inspiration, teaching the faith and its meaning, motivation for Christian action, and a means of creating the memory for the individual and community that sustains them in need, adversity, trial, danger, daily living, and death. Strange it is, indeed, given the strong outreach of the Wesleys among the poor, that this was little celebrated in the songs and hymns of the Wesleyan movement. Even stranger is the reality that Charles Wesley wrote a significant number of hymns with challenging texts for the faith community regarding its service to and among the poor, and most of them were never included in the hymnbooks of Methodism. Richard Heitzenrater maintains: "The hymnody of Methodism does not focus on their work with the poor as much as one might expect, probably because most of the people who were

---

17. *Unpub. Poetry*, 2:102, MS Luke, 104. The poem is based on Luke 7:45: "This woman, since I came in, hath not ceased to kiss my feet."

singing these hymns were the poor themselves." Yet, he goes on to say, "Lines such as, 'Gladly of that little give / Poor thyself, the poor relieve,' are therefore not out of place in that context."[18] Hence, it seems unlikely that the poor themselves were the reason for the exclusion of hymns centered on life and ministry with the poor. Such hymns could well have been sung in the Societies, but they were not. In a number of instances already discussed in this study, Wesley emphasizes in his hymns and poems that the poorest of the poor may still give, as in the case of the widow who gave two coins (Luke 21), of whom Charles wrote:

> God's own mighty power displays,
>   God's own love to sinners shows;
> Free, and disengaged by grace
>   Then the poor her all bestows.

If a congregation tends to mirror the theology of its hymnody and songs, it is important to celebrate life and ministry with and among the poor and marginalized in its singing. This will help provide the metaphors, imagery, and language that will encourage the "constant employment to serve and relieve your Saviour in his poor distressed members" of which Charles Wesley speaks.

One must ask: How will we retain the cognitive capacity to remember the nature of God's grace, its effectiveness among the faithful community, and how will we "use the grace divine"? Memory is a key to Christian identity. Therefore we ask: What will shape our memory? Experiences, events, images, language, rhythm, and music—these molders of memory link us to time, to the past and to the present.

Of course, there are different types of memory—for example, recollective, habitual, experiential, episodic, declarative, and musical. We recall specific information or events. We have habitual recall that motivates the repetition of certain behavior. We remember incidental and extraordinary experiences, often in minute detail. We can often picture each phase of a particular episode in our past. Declarative memory seeks to follow step by step the path to truth about something. We know also that we can distort memory, and we can remember incorrectly.

Memory is crucial to the community of faith, for it has direct social implications. It can guide us to right or wrong action. Therefore, how the community of faith remembers influences its life collectively

---

18. Hetizenrater, *Poor and the People Called Methodists*, 221.

and individually. What the community and individuals decide to do as Christians rests largely on what and how they remember. Unquestionably how individuals remember is very complex, which makes the collective memory of the faith community anything but a simple matter.

In Christian worship and devotion, there are diverse triggers of memory and memory representations. They are important in making us aware of the past and the present, of social responsibility, and of moral obligation. They can lead to direct or indirect awareness of identity and responsibility. Many things will not be remembered without these triggers or representations. They can themselves be filled with content or represent past experiences and events.

The memory created by congregational song can be recollective, habitual, experiential, episodic, and declarative. It shapes communal and individual identity. This is music-enhanced or musical memory. Congregational song includes an added enabler of memory, namely, music with its characteristics of rhythm, meter, tempi, and melody that play decisive roles in enhancing the memory of words, which they accompany. This is illustrated in the Wesleyan tradition by Methodist class meetings, which, as Carlton R. Young notes, "used the singing, recitation, and study of hymns to form a member's faith and prayer, and through tonal memory to inform, recall (*anamnesis*), and sustain between preaching services their faith in the saving power of God in Christ."[19]

In the faith community, there can also be spiritualized memory. In this kind of memory past and present remembrance of ideas, events, and experiences are shaped by certain spiritual markers. For example, if one assumes the view that everything that happens is the will of God, all events and experiences will be remembered through this particular focus.

For the Wesleys, the memory created through song was didactic, inspirational, and motivational. It is unfortunate, given the fact that they saw Christian identity as intimately linked with outreach to the poor, that an important trigger for collective remembering of this identity—namely, congregational song emphasizing life with and among the poor—was essentially omitted from the published corpus of song they shared with the community of faith. This is not to say that Charles Wesley did not create texts that could have been an essential element in shaping communal memory. He did, but only a few of them made their way into the Wesleyan

---

19. Young, *Music of the Heart*, 31.

publications, and those few did not become the hallmarks of Wesleyan song.

IMPLEMENTING A THEOLOGY OF RADICAL GRACE

What must the church do to implement a theology of radical grace that seeks justice for the poor and marginalized? If we follow the example of Charles Wesley, there is a discipline of Christian behavior to be practiced that is motivated by the love of Christ and others.

Labor for the Poor

This is where we begin, and it is decidedly contrary to a view that we must first care for ourselves. It does not suggest that we become negligent of ourselves, families, and friends, but rather that working for the poor becomes integral to the exercise of our vocations and daily lives. This is a radical departure from prevalent life postures, particularly in the West, where education is usually programmed to prepare individuals for specific jobs that will establish them as successful citizens. Often, this is specifically intertwined with a distinct desire for wealth and vocational advancement without any concern for the less fortunate. Even clergy may succumb to this perspective.[20]

The church of which Charles Wesley would be a part, however, would encourage all of its members, regardless of education and vocation, to labor for the poor. This means, as he explicitly says in a previously cited hymn, we must "lay out our gettings [earnings] to relieve / the members of our Lord." Who are the members of our Lord? The poor!

Sacrifice for the Poor

Christians and the church of which they are a part must be willing to sacrifice for the poor. Although they may not realize it, more often than not they pillage the poor by living well, doing little or nothing to alleviate the suffering of the poor. If they are just stewards of what has been entrusted to them, they will consider the poor first and not last. Charles Wesley gives us a standard by which to measure our sacrifice:

20. See above, chapter 3, "The Clergy," 52–56.

> One thing is lacking still[21]
>   But one which all implies,
> To offer up thy heart and will,
>   And life in sacrifice;
>   With gladness to restore
>   Whate'er thy God hath given,
> And thro' his deputies the poor
>   Lay up thy wealth in heaven.

We gladly offer up our hearts, wills, and lives to restore that which God has provided through the poor.

Be a Just Steward

The call to just stewardship is not merely about tithing one's income (a standard 10 percent). In the Wesleyan tradition and in the spirit of Holy Scripture, one lays aside of one's earnings for the poor. This is not an option for the Wesleys, but rather a self-understood mandate. Again, however, one exercises such stewardship not out of obligation but out of love.

Here is a stewardship principle worthy of twenty-first-century practice. Give priority to the poor in budgetary planning as individual Christians and as a church.

Feel the Care of Others

Charles Wesley speaks of feeling the care of others. This is different from merely caring for others. It means establishing a relationship with the poor, which is impossible without personal contact. We will not feel the care of others if we do not visit them and befriend them.

An essential aspect of Christian living is to visit the poor. When one thinks of the contemporary lifestyle of Christians, one must ask: to what extent is visiting the poor[22] important in daily living? How many churches have this dimension of Christian behavior at the heart of their programmatic implementation and budgetary concerns? Most certainly there are individuals and churches that make a concerted effort to reach the poor and marginalized in some manner—through soup kitchens, food banks, housing and employment programs, and prison ministries, to name but a few

---

21. *Unpub. Poetry*, 2:171, MS Luke, 266.

22. On the importance John Wesley placed on visiting the poor, see Maddox, "'Visit the Poor,'" in Heitzenrater, *Poor and the People Called Methodists*, 59–81.

options. Is visiting and caring for the poor truly at the center of Christian living and church life in the twenty-first century? Does any church ask of confirmands and prospective members a response to the question, will you be willing and promise to visit the poor and and learn to feel their care?

Listen to the Poor

It is one thing to visit the poor, to take them baskets of food and clothing, and to supply housing and employment needs, but who will *listen* to them? Listening takes time and patience. To listen to others means that we give full attention to the sound of their voice or the signs of their hands. If we truly listen, we will hear what others are saying, and we are then able to act on or respond to what they have said. The poor need to know that those who they think may not care about them, are making a distinct effort to hear them. In the journey of Christian discipleship, we must be alert and ready to hear what the poor may share with us.

God *hears* the cry of the poor, the homeless, the weak, and the physically challenged. Those who are God's followers must do the same.

Make Friends of the Poor

This is often not an easy task for those who are not poor and do not live in poverty. The global faith community should be reminded continually that the poor need their friendship.

If, as Charles Wesley suggests, the poor are Jesus' bosom-friends, how can Christ's followers avoid befriending them? That would be a travesty! Dare Christians begin each day with a simple one-sentence prayer from Charles? "Help us to make the poor our friends."

Suppose we convert the ideas of the following hymn of Wesley's into a daily prayer for all Christians.

> The poor as Jesus' bosom-friends,[23]
>> The poor he makes his latest care,
> To all his successors commends,
>> And wills us on our hands to bear;
> The poor our dearest care we make,
>> Aspiring to superior bliss,
> And cherish for their Saviour's sake,
>> And love them with a love like his.

---

23. *Unpub. Poetry*, 2:404, MS Acts, 421.

The prayer might read like this: "Lord, you have made the poor your best friends, and their care a first priority, and you have commended their care to us as your will. Help us to make them our best friends, and caring for them our dearest concern, that we might love the poor with a love like yours. Amen." Would the church and its members dare to pray this prayer each day and be willing to personify the fulfillment of the prayer?

Preach the Gospel to the Poor

We have seen time and again that John and Charles Wesley heeded the admonition to share the gospel with the poor. Unquestionably Charles emphasized that it is possible to share the gospel and never speak the word. Nevertheless, in spite of the fact that "actions may speak louder than words," the Wesleys followed the mandate of Holy Scripture to proclaim the saving news of the gospel to everyone, including the poor. They preached good news to the poor, as recorded in their journals and Charles's hymns.

There is a benefit not only for those who may hear the gospel, but also for those who proclaim it. Charles pleads for the change that can come from proclaiming the gospel message to the poor.

> While preaching gospel to the poor,[24]
> My soul impoverish and secure
>   By deep humility;
> Safe in your wounds a novice hide,
> Then shall I preach the Crucified,
>   And nothing know but thee.

Humility is a virtue to be gained by sharing the gospel with the poor. This is a very different perspective from the condescending view of those who might engage in an evangelizing effort in order to help "those poor, unfortunate people" to a better life and salvation in God. Charles knows that they have been chosen first by God, and he can but stand before them in deepest humility as a preacher of the gospel. That is the proper posture for ministry with and among the poor in any age, and most certainly in the twenty-first century.

---

24. *Unpub. Poetry*, 3:49, *MS Preachers* 1786, 9–10, stanza 2 (of six stanzas).

Observe the "Golden Rule"

This seems like very pragmatic advice—do to others as you would have them do to you. Is this not a simple equation for one's moral obligation to oneself and others? It might seem so, but in reviewing Wesley's poem about Mary Naylor's observance of the "golden rule," he describes her motivation to do so: "Justice composed her upright soul, / Justice did all her thoughts control, / And formed her character."

How we respond to others should be motivated and shaped by a deep sense of justice. If the church of today were filled with members whose thoughts were controlled by justice and whose characters were formed by justice, the outreach to and care of the poor and marginalized would be a self-understood matter. Negligence and apathy would be abated. No one would return evil for evil. People would not seek vengeance for injustices done to them. No one would be exploited.

Wesley says, ". . . keep her life in view, / And still her shining steps pursue, / Till all return to God." Would that the church today would do just that!

Welcome Everyone to the Lord's Table

Does this suggest a *carte blanche* invitation to anyone without exception? Is there no justifiable preparation for those who participate in Holy Communion? Are there no restrictions as to who is invited to the Lord's table? Must one be a professed, baptized, or confirmed Christian with membership in a denomination? Who sets the boundaries and requirements? Do we anticipate inviting the poor to the Lord's table and sharing in this meal with them?

If this is the most important meal of which Christians partake, and the one that is the fullest expression of God's loving concern for all humankind, how shall the poor and marginalized know they are welcome there? Holy Communion is the sacrament of love, the communion and fellowship of the body of Christ, and involves participation in the sacrifice of Christ and sharing in his resurrected life. Thus, Holy Communion is a missionary event, a converting ordinance, and signifies in itself the mission of the church. As Petros Vassiliadis avers, "It is only in the eucharist that the church becomes church in its fullest sense."[25] It is the determinant of the church's and the Christian's identity.

At the table of the Lord the community of faith in fellowship with one another through the power of the Holy Spirit is indeed the body of

25. Vassiliadis, *Eucharist and Witness*, 10.

Christ, the church, and has a foretaste of God's kingdom that has come and is yet to come. Thus, Holy Communion is an eschatological meal. It always involves a *becoming.*

What kind of a world does the sacrament help us foresee? It should give us the foresight of Deuteronomy, which when speaking of the sabbatical year of release, anticipates the time when "there shall be no poor" (15:4). Implicit in Deuteronomy's grasp of reality was that there was a giant chasm between the rich and poor, which needed rectification by the "year of release." In the interim, however, the needs of the poor must be addressed by the faithful.

The Bible envisions a society in which there are no poor. It is precisely at the table of the Lord that this vision becomes clearer for the individual and the community of faith. Should not the poor share in this vision?

The well-known early twentieth-century African American poet-pastor Charles Albert Tindley expressed a vision of the forthcoming kingdom of God in which

> No poor are begging on the street,[26]
>> The blind are made to see,
> No homeless wandering soul to meet,
>> Through all eternity.

Is this the vision conveyed at the table of the Lord? Do Tindley's words not remind us that if the kingdom of God is among us, as the New Testament says, this hope of the future should begin its fulfillment in the present?

Pursue "Gospel-Poverty"

This idea is found in only one of Charles Wesley's texts; it is a response to Acts 4:36–37, as noted previously in this study. The biblical account relates the story of the Levite Barnabas, who sold a piece of property and brought the income from the sale as an offering.

> See here an apostolic priest,
>> Commissioned from the sky,
> Who dares of all vain self divest,
>> The needy to supply!

---

26. Stanza 2 of the hymn "There is a land that is free," in Tindley, *Beams of Heaven,* no. 24.

> A primitive example rare
> Of gospel-poverty,
> To feed the flock one's only care,
> And like the Lord to be.

Wesley calls this "A primitive example rare / Of gospel-poverty." As I have noted elsewhere,[27] gospel poverty refers to "complete self-divestment. Gospel poverty is daring to give up all in order to supply the needs of others; to have as one's only care 'to feed the flock.'" For Charles, such action is not an option but is "commissioned from the sky." Why does he speak of it, however, as a rare "primitive example"? He knows that almost no one follows this example in his day.

Charles cannot speak of "gospel-poverty" without relating it to the pursuit of perfection, as he makes clear in the following poem.

1. Wouldst thou require what cannot be?[28]
    The thing impossible to me
        Is possible with God:
    I trust thy truth to make me just,
    Th' omnipotence of love I trust,
        The virtue of thy blood.

2. "Ye shall be perfect" here below
    He spoke it, and it must be so;
        But first he said, "Be poor;
    Hunger, and thirst, repent, and grieve,
    In humble, meek obedience live,
        And labour, and endure.

3. Thus, thus may I the prize pursue,
    And all th' appointed paths pass thro'
        To perfect poverty:
    Thus, let me, Lord, thyself attain,
    And give thee up thine own again,
        Forever lost in thee.

27. Kimbrough, Jr., "Perfection Revisited," in Heitzenrater, *Poor and the People Called Methodists*, 112–13.

28. *Scripture Hymns* (1762), 2:139–40; based on Matt 5:48: "Be ye therefore perfect, even as your Father which is in heaven is perfect."

What is the church today to do with such ideas that link the pursuit of perfection with being poor? One might say, "Most certainly Wesley doesn't mean divestment of all our resources. That would be foolish. And the words *hunger, thirst, repent, grieve, humble, meek obedience, labor,* and *endure* most certainly refer to spiritual enrichment, not self-divestment." That is at best a half-truth. Charles is cautioning all followers of Christ that worldly possessions can get in the way of perfection, for you can pillage the poor by clinging to the things of the world and by refusing to be free of them. Such behavior makes it impossible to discover gospel poverty or perfect poverty. We cannot go on to perfection if we are not willing to be poor. Charles says that he trusts the omnipotence of love, not the omnipotence of wealth.

What is extremely important for the contemporary Christian and for the church is to realize that, even if they are not *of* the world, they are *in* the world; they have a specific social location in time. An appropriate response to that context requires a life posture of willingness to pursue a life of radical grace for the sake of God and others. To commit all of one's resources and those of the church to gospel poverty is a radical departure from personal and corporate greed and the economics of self-investment. It requires tremendous sacrifice.

Where do Christians and the church begin with these radical ideas of Charles Wesley? We begin by examining very seriously how attached we are to worldly things and by considering of what we may divest ourselves for the sake of serving the poor and marginalized. This can be done only if we *remember* our need for gospel poverty and pray faithfully Wesley's words:

> O may I ever be[29]
>> The least in my own eyes,
> *Retain my poverty,*
>> And labour for the prize.

In the final section of this book, one will find a series of worship aids for pastors and worship leaders that will help develop an ethic of service to the poor and an ongoing memory that encourages "constant employment" for the poor and marginalized.

---

29. *Unpub. Poetry,* 2:152. Italics added.

V. Worship Resources for a Theology of Radical Grace[1]

Justice for the Poor and Marginalized

A SUMMONS TO SOCIAL HOLINESS

Call to Worship (L = Lector, P = People)

L: Lo, God is here, let us adore!

P: How awe-inspiring is this place!

L: Let all within us feel the power
   and silent bow before God's face.

**P: Who know this power, God's grace who prove,
   serve God with fear, with reverence love.**

L: Being of beings, may our praise
   your courts with grateful fragrance fill;

P: still may we stand before your face,

L: still hear and do your sovereign will;

**P: to you may all our thoughts a rise,
   ceaseless, accepted sacrifice.**

(Gerhard Tersteegen, Eng. trans. John Wesley)

Hymn   "Come, O holy God and true"   Charles Wesley
Appendix: No. 1, Music:[2] DIX by Conrad Kocher (1838), arr. W. H. Monk (1861)

---

1. Some hymn texts have been modified for use in contemporary worship settings.

2. *UMH*, no. 92. See Kimbrough, Kimbrough, and Young, *Songs for the Poor*, no. 1.

1. Come, O holy God and true!
   Come, and my whole heart renew;
   take me now, possess me whole,
   form the Savior in my soul:
   Refrain

2. In my heart your name reveal,
   stamp me with your Spirit's seal,
   change my nature to divine,
   in me your whole image shine:
   Refrain

3. Be to every sufferer nigh,
   hearing not in vain, the cry
   of the widow in distress,
   of the poor, the fatherless:
   Refrain

4. Raiment give to all that need,
   to the hungry furnish bread,
   to the sick now give relief,
   sooth the hapless prisoners' grief:
   Refrain

5. Love, which wills that all should live,
   Love, which all to all would give,
   Love, that over all prevails,
   Love, that never, never fails:

Refrain:
   Love immense and unconfined,
   Love to all of humankind.

Invocation

Act of Praise, Psalm 12[3]

L: Help, O Lord; no one who is godly is left,
   for the faithful have vanished from humankind.
   They utter lies to each other;
   they speak with flattering lips and a double heart.

P: **May the Lord cut off all flattering lips,**
   the tongue that makes great boasts,
   those who say, "With our tongues we will prevail,
   our lips are our own; who is our master?"

L: The Lord says, "Now I will arise,
   because the poor are plundered,
   because the needy groan;
   I will place them in the safety for which they long."

---

3. Holbert, Kimbrough, and Young, *Psalms for Praise and Worship,* 36–37.

P: The promises of the Lord are promises that are pure,

silver refined in an earthen furnace,

purified seven times.

L: Protect us, O Lord,

guard us from this generation for ever.

P: The wicked prowl on every side,

when vileness is exalted among humankind.

The Scripture for reflection is from the Acts of the Apostles 20:35: "I have showed you all things, how that so labouring ye ought to support the weak, and to remember the words of the Lord Jesus, how he said, 'It is more blessed to give than to receive.'"

After reading these words, Charles Wesley penned what might be called "The Social Manifesto" of the Wesleyan tradition.

1. Your duty let th' Apostle show;
   you ought, you ought to labor so,
       in Jesus' cause employed,
   your calling's works at times pursue,
   and keep the Tentmaker[4] in view,
       and use your hands for God.

2. Work for the weak, and sick and poor,
   raiment and food for them procure,
       and mindful of God's word,
   enjoy the blessedness to give,
   lay out your gettings to relieve
       the members of your Lord.

3. Your labor, which proceeds from love,
   Jesus shall graciously approve,
       with full felicity,
   with brightest crowns your loan repay,
   and tell you in that joyful day,
       "You did it unto Me."

---

4. The Apostle Paul.

Hymn   "Your duty let the Apostle show"   Charles Wesley

Appendix: No. 13, Music:[5] CARRBORO by Timothy E. Kimbrough
Appendix: No. 14, Music[6] by Pablo Sosa

Reflection

One of the most neglected areas of Charles Wesley's poetry is that of his funeral or death hymns—poems written in remembrance of someone who has died and who exemplifies to the community of faith how to live the Christian life.

1. The golden rule she has pursued,
   and did to others as she would
      others should do to her:
   justice composed her upright soul,
   justice did all her thoughts control,
      and formed her character.

2. Affliction, poverty, disease,
   drew out her soul in soft distress,
      the wretched to relieve:
   in all the works of love employed,
   her sympathizing soul enjoyed
      the blessedness to give.

3. Her Savior in his members seen,
   a stranger she received him in,
      an hungry Jesus fed,
   tended her sick, imprisoned Lord,
   and flew in all his wants to afford
      her ministerial aid.

4. A nursing-mother to the poor,
   for them she husbanded her store,
      her life, her all, bestowed;
   for them she labored day and night,
   in doing good her whole delight,
      in copying after God.

5. Away, my tears and selfish sighs!
   The happy saint in paradise
      requires us not to mourn;
   but rather keep her life in view,
   and still her shining steps pursue,
      till all to God return.

Hymn   "The golden rule she has pursued"   Charles Wesley

Appendix: No. 2, Music[7] by Mary K. Jackson
Appendix: No. 3, Music:[8] CORNWALL by Samuel Sebastian Wesley (1872)

---

5. Kimbrough, Kimbrough, and Young, *Songs for the Poor*, no. 10.

6. See Kimbrough and Young, *Help Us to Help Each Other*, 7–9, no. 1.

7. Ibid., no. 9.

8. See Kimbrough, Kimbrough, and Young, *Songs for the Poor*, no. 12.

Prayer for a Social Conscience *(unison)*:

O God, grant us a social conscience in like mind of our forebear in
the faith Charles Wesley, and may his prayer be ours and fulfilled in us:

Your mind throughout my life be shown,
    while listening to the sufferer's cry,
the widow's and the orphan's groan,
    on mercies wings I swiftly fly
the poor and helpless to relieve,
my life, my all for them to give. (Charles Wesley)
    In Christ's holy name we pray. Amen.

The Lord's Prayer and Benediction

A SUMMONS TO STEWARDSHIP OF RESOURCES

Call to Worship (L = Lector, P = People)

L: Happy the multitude
       (but far above our sphere)
    redeemed by Jesus' blood
       from all we covet here!

P: **To him, and to each other joined,**
    They all were of one heart and mind. (Charles Wesley)

L: In this spirit, let us worship God.

Hymn   "Which of the Christians now"   Charles Wesley

Appendix: No. 6, Music: DARWALL'S 148th[9] by John Darwall (1770)
Appendix: No. 7, Music[10] by Ludmila Garbuzova

1.   Which of the Christians now
          would their possessions sell?
       The fact you scarce allow,
          the truth incredible:
      that saints of old so weak should prove
      and as themselves their neighbor love.

2.   Of your abundant store
          you may a few relieve,
       but all to feed the poor
          you cannot, cannot give,
      houses and lands for Christ forego,
      or live as Jesus lived below.

3.   Jesus, your church inspire
          with apostolic love,
       infuse the one desire
          to store our wealth above,
      with earthly goods freely to part
      and joyfully sell all in heart.

9. See *UMH*, no. 715, and Kimbrough, Kimbrough, and Young, *Songs for the Poor*, no. 4.

10. See Kimbrough and Young, *Help Us to Help Each Other*, 29–31, no. 11.

4.   With your pure Spirit filled,
    and loving you alone,
  we shall our substance yield,
    call nothing here our own,
whate'er we have or are submit
and lie, as beggars, at your feet.

Invocation

Act of Praise, Psalm 10:12–18[11]

L: Arise, O Lord; O God, lift up your hand;
    forget not the afflicted.

P: **Why do the wicked renounce God,
    and say in their hearts, "You will not call to account"?**

L: You indeed see, you note trouble and vexation,
    that you may take it into your hands;

P: **the unfortunate commit themselves to you;
    you have been the helper of the orphan.**

L: Break the arm of the wicked and evildoers;

P: **seek out their wickedness till you find none.**

L: The Lord is Ruler for ever and ever;

P: **the nations shall perish from God's land.**

L: O Lord, you will hear the desire of the meek,
    you will strengthen their hearts;

P: **you will incline your ear
    to do justice to the orphan and the oppressed,
    so that people on earth may strike terror no more.**

Lector 1: The first Scripture for reflection in this service is Acts of the Apostles 4:32: "The multitude of them that believed, were of one heart, and one soul: neither said any of them, that aught of the things which he possessed, was his own, but they had all things in common. Neither was there any among them that lacked."

11. Holbert, Kimbrough, and Young, *Psalms for Praise and Worship*, 36.

Charles Wesley once read these words and wrote the hymn "Happy the Multitude," the first stanza of which we read at the opening of this service. The hymn was unpublished at Wesley's death. It reflects a keen understanding of what it means to belong to Christian community.

Hymn   "Happy the Multitude"   Charles Wesley

Appendix: No. 15, Music[12] by Carlton R. Young

1.   Happy the multitude
          (but far above our sphere)
       redeemed by Jesus' blood
          from all we covet here!
    To him, and to each other joined,
    they all were of one heart and mind.

2.   His blood the cement was
          who died on Calvary,
       and fastened to his cross
          they could not disagree:
    One soul did all the members move,
    the soul of harmony and love.

3.   Their goods were free for all,
          appropriated to none,
       while none presumed to call
          what he possessed his own;
    the diff'rent base of *thine* and *mine*
    was lost in charity divine.

4.   No overplus, or need,
          no rich or poor were there,
       content with daily bread
          where all enjoyed their share;
    with every common blessing blessed
    they nothing had, yet all possessed.

Lector 2: A second Scripture passage for reflection is also from the Acts of the Apostles 4:36-37: "And Joses, who by the apostles was surnamed Barnabas, (which is being interpreted, the son of consolation,) a Levite,

12. See Kimbrough and Young, *Help Us to Help Each Other*, 37–39, no. 13.

and of the country of Cyprus, having land, sold it, and brought the money, and laid it at the apostles' feet." Let us join in singing Charles Wesley's response to this text.

Hymn   "You pastors hired who undertake"   Charles Wesley

Appendix: No. 12, Music[13] by Timothy E. Kimbrough
Appendix: No. 16, Music:[14] KINGSFOLD, English traditional melody

1. You pastors hired who undertake
       the aweful ministry
   for lucre or ambition's sake,
       a nobler pattern see!
   Who greedily your pay receive,
       and adding cure to cure,
   in splendid ease and pleasures live
       by pillaging the poor.

2. See here an apostolic priest,
       commissioned from the sky,
   who dares of all vain self divest,
       the needy to supply!
   A primitive example rare
       of gospel-poverty,
   to feed the flock one's only care,
       and like the Lord to be.

3. Jesus, to us apostles raise,
       like-minded pastors give
   who freely may dispense your grace
       as freely they receive;
   who disengaged from all below
       may earthly things despise,
   and every creature-good forego
       for treasure in the skies.

Reflection on Charles Wesley's Words

Prayer and Benediction

13. See Kimbrough and Young, *Help Us to Help Each Other*, 11–13, no. 3.

14. See *UMH*, no. 179, and Kimbrough, Kimbrough, and Young, *Songs for the Poor*, no. 9.

A SUMMONS TO ACTS OF MERCY

Call to Worship

Hymn   "Help us to help each other, Lord"   Charles Wesley

Appendix: No. 10, Music:[15] ST. AGNES by John B. Dykes (1866)
Appendix: No. 11, Music[16] by David Plüss

1. Help us to help each other, Lord,
   each other's cross to bear,
   let all their friendly aid afford,
   and feel each other's care.

2. Help us to build each other up,
   our little stock improve;
   increase our faith, confirm our hope,
   and perfect us in love.

3. Thus let the fullest joy be given,
   the same delight we prove,
   in earth, in paradise, in heaven,
   our all in all is love.

4. Then, when the mighty work is
   wrought,
   receive your ready bride;
   give us in heaven a happy lot
   with all the sanctified.

Collect for the Day (*unison*):

Unite the pair so long disjoined,
   Knowledge and vital piety,
Learning and holiness combined
   And truth and love let each one see
In these whom up to You we give,
   Yours, wholly yours to die and live. (Charles Wesley)
      In Christ's name, Amen.

Act of Praise, Psalm 19[17]

L: The heavens are telling the glory of God;
   and the firmament proclaims God's handiwork.

P: **Day to day pours forth speech,**
   and night to night declares knowledge.

---

15. See *UMH*, no. 561, and Kimbrough, Kimbrough, and Young, *Songs for the Poor*, no. 2.

16. See Kimbrough and Young, *Help Us to Help Each Other*, 10–11, no. 2.

17. Holbert, Kimbrough, and Young, *Psalms for Praise and Worship*, 43–44.

L: There is no speech, nor are there words;
their voice is not heard;

**P: yet their voice goes out through all the earth,
and their words to the end of the world.**

L: In them God has set a tent for the sun,
which comes forth like a bridegroom leaving his chamber,
and runs its course with joy like a strong man.

**P: Its rising is from the end of the heavens,
and its circuit to the end of them;
and there is nothing hid from its heat.**

L: The law of the Lord is perfect,
reviving the soul;

**P: the testimony of the Lord is sure,
making wise the simple;**

L: the precepts of the Lord are right,
rejoicing the heart;

**P: the commandment of the Lord is pure,
enlightening the eyes;**

L: the fear of the Lord is clean, enduring for ever;

**P: the ordinances of the Lord are true,
and righteous altogether.**

L: More to be desired are they than gold,
even much fine gold;

**P: sweeter also than honey
and drippings of the honeycomb.**

L: Moreover by them is your servant warned;
in keeping them there is great reward.

**P: But who can understand one's own errors?
Clear me from hidden faults.**

L: Also keep your servant from the insolent;
let them not have dominion over me!

**P: Then I shall be blameless,
and innocent of great transgression.
Let the words of my mouth and the meditation of my heart**

be acceptable in your sight,
O Lord, my Rock and my Redeemer.

Lector 1: The following verse of Scripture is for our reflection: "Be therefore perfect, even as your Father in heaven is perfect" (Matt 5:48:). In
responding to this text, Charles Wesley wrote the hymn "Wouldst thou
require what cannot be?" What can Wesley mean in stanza 3 that we
"pass through to perfect poverty"?

Hymn   "Would you require what cannot be?"   Charles Wesley

Appendix: No. 8, Music[18] MERIBAH by Lowell Mason (1839)
Appendix: No. 9, Music[19] by I-to Loh

1. Would you require what cannot be?
    The thing impossible for me
        is possible with God:
    I trust your truth to make me just,
    the omnipotence of love I trust,
        the virtue of your blood.

2. "You shall be perfect" here below,
    he spoke it and it must be so;
        but first he said, "Be poor;
    hunger, and thirst, repent, and grieve,
    in humble, meek obedience live,
        and labor, and endure."

3. Thus, thus may I the prize pursue,
    and all the appointed paths pass through
        to perfect poverty:
    thus, let me, Lord, yourself attain,
    and give to you your own again
        that lost in you I'll be.

Lector 2: The second verse of Scripture for reflection is Luke 16:9: "And I
tell you, make friends for yourselves by means of unrighteous mammon,
so that when it fails they may receive you into the eternal habitations."

18. See Kimbrough, Kimbrough, and Young, *Songs for the Poor*, no 7.
19. See Kimbrough and Young, *Help Us to Help Each Other*, 42–43, no. 15.

In pondering these words, Charles Wesley shaped a prayer for wisdom, diligence, and justice unique in the Wesleyan literature. It should be the constant prayer of all who seek the unity of knowledge, vital piety, and acts of mercy.

> Whate'er you shall to us entrust,
> with your peculiar blessing blessed,
> O make us diligent and just,
> as stewards faithful to the least,
> endowed with wisdom to possess
> the mammon of unrighteousness.

Hymn   "The poor as Jesus' bosom friends"   Charles Wesley

Appendix: No. 4, Music:[20] O WALY WALY, adapt. and arr. Carlton R. Young
Appendix: No. 5, Music:[21] ST. CATHERINE by Henri F. Hemy (1864)

1. The poor as Jesus' bosom-friends,
   the poor he makes his latest care,
   to all his followers commends,
   and wills us on our hands to bear;
   the poor our dearest care we make,
   and love them for our Savior's sake.

2. Whatever you to us entrust,
   with your peculiar blessing blessed,
   O make us diligent and just,
   as stewards faithful to the least,
   endowed with wisdom to possess
   the mammon of unrighteousness.

3. Help us to make the poor our friends,
   by that which paves the way to hell,
   that when our loving labor ends,
   and dying from this earth we fail,
   our friends may greet us in the skies
   born to a life that never dies.

Prayer and Benediction

---

20. See Kimbrough and Young, *Help Us to Help Each Other,* 18–19, no. 6.

21. See *UMH*, no. 710, and Kimbrough, Kimbrough, and Young, *Songs for the Poor,* no. 3.

Appendix

Musical Settings for Congregational Singing
for Liturgies 1–3

The texts in the hymn settings of the Appendix have been edited in contemporary style for congregational singing. The sources of the original texts are cited on the first page of each hymn. They are available at the following website:http://www.divinity.duke.edu/initiatives-centers/cswt/wesley-texts/manuscript-verse. The PDFs of the liturgies in chapter V and the hymn selections in the Appendix may be downloaded for one-time use at the following website: http://www.stkimbrough.com.

1

Come, O holy God and true

1. Come, O ho-ly God and true! Come, and my whole heart re-new;
2. In my heart your name re-veal, stamp me with your Spir-it's seal,
3. Be to eve-ry suf-ferer nigh, hear-ing, not in vain, the cry
4. Rai-ment give to all that need, to the hun-gry fur-nish bread,
5. Love, which wills that all should live, Love, which all to all would give,

take me now, pos-sess me whole, form the Sav-ior in my soul:
change my na-ture to di-vine, in me your whole i-mage shine:
of the wi-dow in dis-tress, soothe the hap-less fa-ther-less:
to the sick now give re-lief, soothe the hap-less pri-soners' grief:
Love, that o-ver all pre-vails, Love, that nev-er, nev-er fails.

Refrain

Love im-mense and un-con-fined, Love to all of hu-man-kind.

WORDS: Charles Wesley, *HSP* (1749), 1:38-9, No. 8; the stanzas for this hymn were selected by author of this volume from a 162-line poem titled "The Beatitudes," based on Matthew 5:3-12; stanzas 1-2 = lines 97-104; stanzas 3-4 = lines 133-40; stanza 5 = lines 115-18; the refrain = lines 113-14. A seven-stanza version (including the five stanzas above) of this hymn was first published by S T Kimbrough, Jr., in 1993.
MUSIC: Conrad Kocher (1838), DIX, arr. W. H. Monk (1861)

1. Come, O holy God and true!
   Come, and my whole heart renew;
   take me now, possess me whole,
   form the Savior in my soul:
   Refrain:

2. In my heart your name reveal,
   stamp me with your Spirit's seal,
   change my nature to divine,
   in me your whole image shine:
   Refrain:

3. Be to every sufferer nigh,
   hearing, not in vain, the cry
   of the widow in distress,
   of the poor, the fatherless:
   Refrain:

4. Raiment give to all that need,
   to the hungry furnish bread,
   to the sick now give relief,
   soothe the hapless prisoners' grief:
   Refrain:

5. Love, which wills that all should live,
   Love, which all to all would give,
   Love, that over all prevails,
   Love, that never, never fails.
   Refrain:
   Love immense and unconfined,
   Love to all of humankind.

2 The golden rule she has pursued

♩ = 96-100

1. The gold - en rule she has pur - sued, and
2. Af - flic - tion, pov - er - ty, dis - ease, drew
3. Her Sav - ior in his mem - bers seen, a
4. A nurs - ing moth - er to the poor, for
5. A - way my tears and sel - fish sighs! The

did to oth - ers as she would oth - ers
out her soul in soft dis - tress, the
stran - ger she re - ceived him in, an
them she hus - band - ed her store, her
hap - py saint in par - a - dise re -

should do to her:
wretch - ed to re - lieve:
hun - gry Je - sus fed,
life, her all, be - stowed;
quires us not to mourn;

WORDS: Charles Wesley, *Funeral Hymns* (1759); the stanzas for this hymn were selected by the author of this volume from the poem "On the Death of Mrs. Mary Naylor, March 21st, 1757"; stanza 1 is from Part II (original stanza 3), p. 51; stanzas 2-3 from Part III (original stanzas 2-4), p. 53; stanza 5 from Part I (original stanza 2), pp. 49-50.
MUSIC: Mary K. Jackson

jus - tice com - posed her up - right soul, jus - tice did all her
in all the works of love em - ployed, her sym - pa - thiz - ing
tend - ed her sick, im - pris - oned Lord, and flew in all his
for them she la - bored day and night, in do - ing good her
but rath - er keep her life in view, and still her shin - ing

thoughts con - trol, and formed her char - ac - ter.
soul en - joyed the bless - ed - ness to give.
wants to af - ford her min - is - te - rial aid.
whole de - light, in copy - ing af - ter God.
steps pur - sue, till all to God re - turn.

1. The golden rule she has pursued,
   and did to others as she would
   others should do to her:
   justice composed her upright soul,
   justice did all her thoughts control,
   and formed her character.

2. Affliction, poverty, disease,
   drew out her soul in soft distress,
   the wretched to relieve:
   in all the works of love employed,
   her sympathizing soul enjoyed
   the blessedness to give.

3. Her Savior in his members seen,
   a stranger she received him in,
   an hungry Jesus fed,
   tended her sick, imprisoned Lord,
   and flew in all his wants to afford
   her ministerial aid.

4. A nursing-mother to the poor,
   for them she husbanded her store,
   her life, her all, bestowed;
   for them she labored day and night,
   in doing good her whole delight,
   in copying after God.

5. Away my tears and selfish sighs!
   The happy saint in paradise
   requires us not to mourn;
   but rather keep her life in view,
   and still her shining steps pursue,
   till all to God return.

115

3   The golden rule she has pursued

1. The gold-en rule she has pur-sued and did to oth-ers
2. Af-flict-ion, pov-er-ty, dis-ease, drew out her soul in
3. Her Sav-ior in his mem-bers seen a strang-er she re-
4. A nurs-ing mo-ther to the poor, for them she hus-band-
5. A-way, my tears and self-ish sighs! The hap-py saint in

as she would oth - ers should do to her: jus -
soft dis-tress, the wretch-ed to re - lieve: in
ceived him in, an hun-gry Je - sus fed, tend -
ed her store, her life, her all be - stowed; for
par-a-dise re - quires us not to mourn; but

tice com-posed her up-right soul, jus - tice did all her
all the works of love em-ployed, her sym-pa-thiz-ing
ed her sick, im - pri-soned Lord, and flew in all his
them she la-bored day and night, in do - ing good her
ra-ther keep her life in view, and still her shin-ing

WORDS: Charles Wesley, *Funeral Hymns* (1759); the stanzas for this hymn were selected by the author of this
volume from the poem "On the Death of Mrs. Mary Naylor, March 21st, 1757"; stanza 1 is from Part II (original
stanza 3), p. 51; stanzas 2-3 from Part III (original stanzas 2-4), p. 53; stanza 5 from Part I (original stanza 2), pp.
49-50.
MUSIC: Samuel Sebastian Wesley (1872), CORNWALL

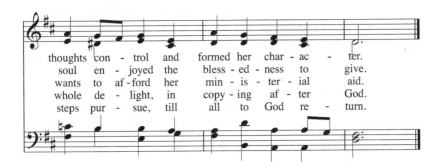

thoughts con - trol and formed her char - ac - ter.
soul en - joyed the bless - ed - ness to give.
wants to af - ford her min - is - ter - ial aid.
whole de - light, in copy - ing af - ter God.
steps pur - sue, till all to God re - turn.

1. The golden rule she has pursued,
   and did to others as she would
   others should do to her:
   justice composed her upright soul,
   justice did all her thoughts control,
   and formed her character.

2. Affliction, poverty, disease,
   drew out her soul in soft distress,
   the wretched to relieve:
   in all her works of love employed
   her sympathizing soul enjoyed
   the blessedness to give.

3. Her Savior in his members seen,
   a stranger she received him in,
   an hungry Jesus fed,
   tended her sick, imprisoned Lord,
   and flew in all his wants to afford
   her ministerial aid.

4. A nursing-mother to the poor,
   for them she husbanded her store,
   her life, her all, bestowed;
   for them she labored day and night,
   in doing good her whole delight,
   in copying after God.

5. Away, my tears and selfish sighs!
   The happy saint in paradise
   requires us not to mourn;
   but rather keep her life in view,
   and still her shining steps pursue,
   till all to God return.

4

The poor as Jesus' bosom-friends

$\bullet$ = 62

1. The poor as Je - sus' bos - om friends, the poor he
makes his lat - est care, to all his fol - low - ers com - mends, and wills us on our hands to bear; the poor our

2. What - ev - er you to us en - trust, with your pe - cu - liar bless - ing blessed, O make us dil - i - gent and just, as stew - ards faith - ful to the least, en - dowed with

3. Help us to make the poor our friends, by that which paves the way to hell, that when our lov - ing la - bor ends, and dy - ing from this earth we fail, our friends may

WORDS: Charles Wesley, stanza 1 (alt.), MS Acts, p. 421; stanzas 2 and 3, MS Luke, pp. 223-23; in *Unpub. Poetry*, 2:404, 157.
MUSIC: O WALY WALY, English folk melody, adapt. and arr., Carlton R. Young

Music adapt. and arr. © 2010 Carlton R. Young. Used by permission.

dear - est care we make, and love them for our Sav - ior's sake.
wis - dom to pos - sess the mam - mon of un - right - eous -ness.
greet us in the skies born to a life that nev - er dies.

Acts 20:35-6: I have showed you all things, how that so laboring ye ought to support the weak, and to remember the words of the Lord Jesus, how he said, it is more blessed to give than to receive. And when he had thus spoken, he kneeled down, and prayed with them all.

Luke 16:9: And I say unto you, Make to yourselves friends of the mammon of unright-eousness; that, when ye fail, they may receive you into everlasting habitations.

1. The poor as Jesus' bosom friends,
    the poor he makes his latest care,
  to all his followers commends,
    and wills us on our hands to bear;
  the poor our dearest care we make,
  and love them for our Savior's sake.

2. Whatever you to us entrust,
    with your peculiar blessing blessed,
  O make us diligent and just,
    as stewards faithful to the least,
  endowed with wisdom to possess
  the mammon of unrighteousness.

3. Help us to make the poor our friends,
    by that which paves the way to hell,
  that when our loving labor ends,
    and dying from this earth we fail,
  our friends may greet us in the skies
  born to a life that never dies.

5   The poor as Jesus' bosom-friends

1. The poor as Je - sus' bo - som
2. What - e - ver you to us en -
3. Help us to make the poor our

friends, the poor he makes his lat - est
trust, with your pe - cu - liar bless - ing
friends, by that which paves the way to

care, to all his fol - ow - ers com -
blessed, O make us dil - i - gent and
hell, that when our lov - ing la - bor

mends, and wills us on our hands to
just, as stew - ards faith - ful to the
ends, and dy - ing from this earth we

WORDS: Charles Wesley, stanza 1 (alt.), MS Acts, p. 421; stanzas 2 and 3, MS Luke, pp. 223-24; in *Unpub. Poetry*, 2:404, 157.
MUSIC: Henri F. Hemy (1864), ST. CATHERINE, adapt. James G. Walton (1874)

bear; the poor our dear - est care we
least, en - dowed with wis - dom to pos -
fail, our friends may greet us in the

make, and love them for our Sav - ior's sake.
sess the mam-mon of un - right - eous - ness.
skies born to a life that nev - er dies.

Acts 20:35-6: I have showed you all things, how that so laboring ye ought to support the weak, and to remember the words of the Lord Jesus, how he said, it is more blessed to give than to receive. And when he had thus spoken, he kneeled down, and prayed with them all.

Luke 16:9: And I say unto you, Make to yourselves friends of the mammon of unrighteousness; that, when ye fail, they may receive you into everlasting habitations.

1. The poor as Jesus' bosom friends,
   the poor he makes his latest care,
   to all his followers commends,
   and wills us on our hands to bear;
   the poor our dearest care we make,
   and love them for our Savior's sake.

2. Whatever you to us entrust,
   with your peculiar blessing blessed,
   O make us diligent and just,
   as stewards faithful to the least,
   endowed with wisdom to possess
   the mammon of unrighteousness.

3. Help us to make the poor our friends,
   by that which paves the way to hell,
   that when our loving labor ends,
   and dying from this earth we fail,
   our friends may greet us in the skies
   born to a life that never dies.

6 Which of the Christians now

1. Which of the Christ - ians now would
2. Of your a - bund - ant store you
3. Je - sus, your church in - spire with
4. With your pure Spir - it filled, and

their pos - sess - ions sell? The fact you scarce al -
may a few re - lieve, but all to feed the
a - pos - tol - ic love, in - fuse the one de -
lov - ing you a - lone, we shall our sub - stance

low, the truth in - cred - i - ble: that
poor you can - not, can - not give, hous -
sire to store our wealth a - bove, with
yield, call noth - ing here our own, what -

saints of old so weak should prove and
es and lands for Christ fore - go, or
earth - ly goods free - ly to part and
e'er we have or are sub - mit and

WORDS: Charles Wesley, MS Acts, pp. 74-5, in *Unpub. Poetry*, 2:197-98.
MUSIC: John Darwall (1770), DARWALL'S 148th; harm. *Hymns Ancient and Modern* (1861)

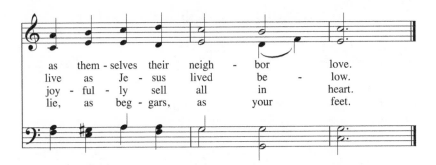

as	them - selves their	neigh - bor	love.
live	as Je - sus	lived be -	low.
joy - ful - ly	sell all	in	heart.
lie,	as beg - gars,	as your	feet.

Acts 4:34-5: Neither was there any among them that lacked: for as many as were possessors of lands or houses sold them, and brought the prices of the things that were sold, and laid them down at the apostles' feet: and distribution was made unto each as any had need.

1. Which of the Christians now
   would their possessions sell?
   The fact you scarce allow,
   the truth incredible:
   that saints of old so weak should prove
   and as themselves their neighbor love.

2. Of your abundant store
   you may a few relieve,
   but all to feed the poor
   you cannot, cannot give,
   houses and lands for Christ forego,
   or live as Jesus lived below.

3. Jesus, your church inspire
   with apostolic love,
   infuse the one desire
   to store our wealth above,
   with earthly goods freely to part,
   and joyfully sell all in heart.

4. With your pure Spirit filled,
   and loving you alone,
   we shall our substance yield,
   call nothing here our own,
   whate'er we have or are submit
   and lie, as beggars, at your feet.

7 Which of the Christians now

♩ = 112

1. Which of the Chris - tians now would their pos - sess - ions sell? The fact you scarce al - low, the
2. Of your a - bun - dant store you may a few re - lieve, but all to feed the poor you
3. Je - sus, your church in - spire with a - pos - tol - ic love, in - fuse the one de - sire to
4. With your pure Spir - it filled, and lov - ing you a - lone, we shall our sub - stance yield, call

WORDS: Charles Wesley, MS Acts, pp. 74-5, in *Unpub. Poetry,* 2:197-98.
MUSIC: Ludmila Pavlovna Garbuzova

truth in - cre - di - ble: that
can - not, can - not give, hous -
store our wealth a - bove, with
noth - ing here our own, what -

saints of old so weak should prove and
es and lands for Christ fore - go, or
earth - ly goods free - ly to part, and
e'er we have or are sub - mit and

as them - selves their neigh - bor love.
live as Je - sus lived be - low.
joy - ful - ly sell all in heart.
lie, as beg - gars, at your feet.

Which of the Chris - tians now would

their pos - sess - ions sell?

Acts 4:34-5: Neither was there any among them that lacked: for as many as were possessors of lands or houses sold them, and brought the prices of the things that were sold, and laid them down at the apostles' feet: and distribution was made unto each as any had need.

1. Which of the Christians now
        would their possessions sell?
    The fact you scarce allow,
        the truth incredible:
    that saints of old so weak should prove
    and as themselves their neighbor love.

2. Of your abundant store
        you may a few relieve,
    but all to feed the poor
        you cannot, cannot give,
    houses and lands for Christ forego,
    or live as Jesus lived below.

3. Jesus, your church inspire
        with apostolic love,
    infuse the one desire
        to store our wealth above,
    with earthly goods freely to part,
    and joyfully sell all in heart.

4. With your pure Spirit filled,
        and loving you alone,
    we shall our substance yield,
        call nothing here our own,
    whate'er we have or are submit
    and lie, as beggars, at your feet.

Would you require what cannot be? 8

1. Would you re-quire what can-not be? The thing im-pos-si-ble to me is pos-si-ble with God: I trust your truth to make me just, the om-ni-po-tence of God I trust, the vir-tue of your blood.

2. "You shall be per-fect" here be-low, he spoke it and it must be so; but first he said, "Be poor; hun-ger, and thirst, re-pent, and grieve, hum-ble, meek o-be-dience live, and la-bor, and en-dure."

3. Thus, thus may I the prize pur-sue, and all the ap-point-ed ways pass through to per-fect pov-er-ty: thus, let me, Lord, your-self at-tain, and give you up your own a-gain, that lost in you I'll be.

WORDS: Charles Wesley, *Scripture Hymns* (1762), 2:139-40.
MUSIC: Lowell Mason (1939), MERIBAH

9   Would you require what cannot be?

♩ = 69 Unison

1. Would you re - quire what can - not be? The thing im -
2. "You shall be per - fect" here be - low, he spoke it,
3. Thus, thus may I the prize pur - sue, and all the ap -

pos - si - ble to me is pos - si -
and it must be so; but first he
point - ed paths pass through to per - fect

ble with God.
said, "Be poor;
pov - er - ty:

I trust your truth to make me just, the om -
hun - ger, and thirst, re - pent, and grieve, in
thus, let me, Lord, your - self at - tain, and

WORDS: Charles Wesley, *Scripture Hymns* (1762), 2:139-40.
MUSIC: I-to Loh

ni - po - tence of love I trust, the
hum - ble, meek o - be - dience live, and
give you up your own a - gain, that

vir - tue of your blood.
la - bor, and en - dure."

lost in you I'll be.

Matthew 5:48: Be ye therefore perfect, even as your Father in heaven is perfect.

1. Would you require what cannot be?
   The thing impossible to me
     is possible with God.
   I trust your truth to make me just,
   the omnipotence of love I trust,
     the virtue of your blood.

2. "You shall be perfect" here below,
   he spoke it, and it must be so;
     but first he said, "Be poor;
   hunger, and thirst, repent, and grieve,
   in humble, meek obedience live,
     and labor, and endure."

3. Thus, thus may I the prize pursue,
and all the appointed paths pass through
    to perfect poverty:
thus, let me, Lord, yourself attain,
and give you up your own again,
    that lost in you I'll be.

10 Help us to help each other, Lord

1. Help us to help each oth - er,
   Lord, each oth - er's cross to bear,
   let all their friend - ly aid af -
   ford, and feel each oth - er's care.

2. Help us to build each oth - er
   up, our lit - tle stock im - prove;
   in - crease our faith, con - firm our
   hope, and per - fect us in love.

3. Thus let the full - est joy be
   given, the same de - light we prove,
   in earth, in par - a - dise,
   heaven, our all in all is love.

4. Then, when the migh - ty work is
   wrought, re - ceive your read - y bride;
   give us in heaven a hap - py
   lot with all the sanc - ti - fied.

WORDS; Charles Wesley, *HSP* (1742), from a four-part poem titled "A Prayer for Persons joined in Fellowship," pp. 83-7; stanzas 1-2, 4 are original stanzas 3-4, 6 of Part I (p. 83) and stanza 3 (alt.) is original stanza 9 of Part IV (p. 87). These stanzas have appeared in some hymnals with the original stanzas 1 and 2. Stanza 1 of the original text begins "Try us, O God, and search the ground."
MUSIC: John B. Dykes, ST. AGNES

Help us to help each other, Lord 11

1. Help us to help each oth - er, Lord, each oth - er's cross to bear, let all their friend - ly aid af - ford, and feel each oth - er's,
2. Help us to build each oth - er up, our lit - tle stock im - prove; in - crease our faith, con - firm our hope, and per - fect us, and
3. Thus let our full - est joy be given, the same de - light we prove, in earth, in par - a - dise, in heaven, our all in all is,
4. Then, when the might - y work is wrought, re - ceive your read - y bride; give us in heaven a hap - py lot with all the sanc - ti,

WORDS: Charles Wesley, *HSP* (1742), from a four-part poem titled "A Prayer for Persons joined in Fellow-ship," pp. 83-7; stanzas 1-2, 4 are original stanzas 3-4, 6 of Part I (p. 83) and stanza 3 (alt.) is original stanza 9 of Part IV (p. 87). Stanza 1 of the original text begins, "Try us, O God, and search the ground."
MUSIC: David Plüss

feel | each | oth - er's, | feel | each | oth - er's | care.
per - | fect | us, and | per - | fect | us in | love.
all | in | all is, | all | in | all is | love.
all | the | sanc - ti, | all | the | sanc - ti - | fied.

1. Help us to help each other, Lord,
    each other's cross to bear,
    let all their friendly aid afford,
    and feel each other's care.

2. Help us to build each other up,
    our little stock improve;
    increase our faith, confirm our hope,
    and perfect us in love.

3. Thus let our fullest joy be given,
    the same delight we prove,
    in earth, in paradise, in heaven,
    our all in all is love.

4. Then, when the mighty work is wrought,
    receive your ready bride;
    give us in heaven a happy lot
    with all the sanctified.

You pastors hired who undertake 12

1. You | pas - tors | hired | who | un - der - take | the
2. See | here | an | a - pos - | tol - ic | priest, | com -
3. Je - | sus, | to | us | a - pos - tles | raise, | like -

WORDS: Charles Wesley, MS Acts, p. 75, in *Unpub. Poetry*, 2:298-99.
MUSIC: Timothy E. Kimbrough

Music © 2010 The Charles Wesley Society, Archives and History Center, Drew University, 36 Madison Avenue, Madison, NJ 07940. All rights reserved. Used by permission.

awe - ful min - is - try   for   lu - cre or am -
mis - sioned from the sky,   who   dares of all vain
mind - ed pas - tors give   who   free - ly may dis -

bi - tion's sake, a   no - bler pat - tern see!   Who
self di - vest, the   need - y to sup - ply!   A
pense your grace as   free - ly they re - ceive;   who

greed - i - ly your pay re - ceive, and   add - ing cure to
prim - i - tive ex - am - ple rare of   gos - pel pov - er -
dis - en - gaged from all be - low may   earth - ly things des -

cure,   in   splen - did   ease   and   plea - sures   live   by
ty,   to   feed   the   flock   one's   on - ly   care,   and
pise,   and   eve - ry   crea - ture   - good   fore - go   for

pil - lag - ing   the   poor.
like   the   Lord   to   be.
treas - ure   in   the   skies.

Acts 4:36-7: And Joses, who by the apostles was surnamed Barnabas (which is being interpreted, the son of consolation), a Levite, and of the country of Cyprus, having land, sold it, and brought the money, and laid it at the apostles' feet.

1. You pastors hired who undertake
    the aweful ministry
  for lucre or ambition's sake,
    a nobler pattern see!
Who greedily your pay receive,
    and adding cure to cure,
in splendid ease and pleasure's live
    by pillaging the poor.

2. See here an apostolic priest,
    commissioned from the sky,
who dares of all vain self divest,
    the needy to supply!
A primitive example rare
    of gospel-poverty,
to feed the flock one's only care,
    and like the Lord to be.

3. Jesus, to us apostles raise,
    like-minded pastors give
who freely may dispense your grace
    as freely they receive;
who disengaged from all below
    may earthly things despise,
and every creature-good forego
    for treasure in the skies.

Your duty let th' Apostle show **13**

1. Your du-ty let th' A-pos-tle show; you ought, you ought to la-bor so, in Je-sus' cause em-ployed, your call-ing's works at times pur-sue, and keep A-pos-tle Paul* in view, and use your hands for God.

2. Work for the weak, and sick, and poor, rai-ment and food for them pro-cure, and mind-ful of God's word, en-joy the bless-ed-ness to give, lay out your get-tings to re-lieve the mem-bers of your Lord.

3. Your la-bor which pro-ceeds from love, Je-sus shall gra-cious-ly ap-prove, with full fe-li-ci-ty, with bright-est crowns your loan re-pay, and tell you in that joy-ful day, "You did it un-to Me."

* the apostle Paul = the tent-maker in the first printing

WORDS: Charles Wesley, MS Acts, from *Unpub. Poetry*, 2:403-4, stanza 1.
MUSIC: Timothy E. Kimbrough, CARRBORO

135

14   Your duty let th' Apostle show

Refrain

Your du - ty, your du - ty, let the A - pos - tle your

du - ty show; your du - ty, your du - ty

WORDS: Charles Wesley, from MS Acts in *Unpub. Poetry,* 2:403-4, stanza 1 alt.
MUSIC: Pablo Sosa

136

let the A-pos-tle show.

1. Your du - ty let th' A-
2. Work for the weak, and
3. Your la - bor, which pro -

pos - tle show, you ought, you ought to la - bor so in
sick, and poor, rai - ment and food for them pro - cure, and
ceeds from love, Je - sus shall gra - cious - ly ap - prove, with

Je - sus' cause em - ployed, your call - ing's works at
mind - ful of God's word, en - joy the bless - ed -
full fe - li - ci - ty, with bright - est crowns your

times pur - sue, and keep A - pos - tle Paul in view and
ness to give, lay out your get - tings to re - lieve the
loan re - pay, and tell you in that joy - ful day, "You

G   Am   G

use your hands for God.
mem - bers of your Lord.
did it un - to Me."

C   D7   G

Acts 20:35: I have showed you all things, how that so laboring ye ought to support the weak, and to remember the words of the Lord Jesus, how he said, "It is more blessed to give than to receive."

1. Your duty let th' Apostle show;
   you ought, you ought to labor so,
     in Jesus' cause employed,
   your calling's works at times pursue,
   and keep Apostle Paul in view,
     and use your hands for God.

2. Work for the weak, and sick, and poor,
   raiment and food for them procure,
     and mindful of God's word,
   enjoy the blessedness to give,
   lay out your gettings to relieve
     the members of your Lord.

3. Your labor, which proceeds from love,
   Jesus shall graciously approve,
     with full felicity,
   with brightest crowns your loan repay,
   and tell you in that joyful day,
     "You did it unto Me."

Happy the multitude

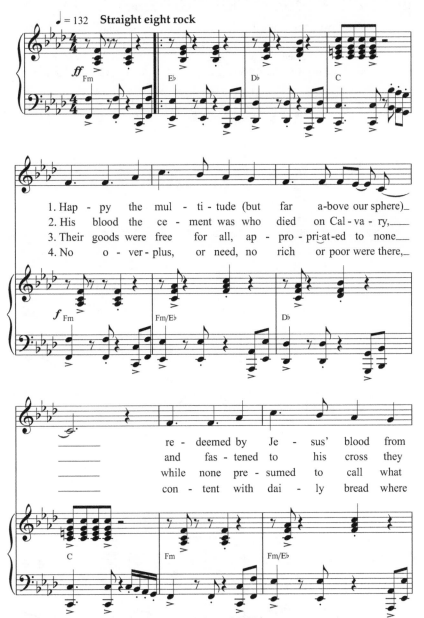

1. Hap - py the mul - ti - tude (but far a - bove our sphere)__ re - deemed by Je - sus' blood from
2. His blood the ce - ment was who died on Cal - va - ry,__ and fas - tened to his cross they
3. Their goods were free for all, ap - pro - pri - at - ed to none__ while none pre - sumed to call what
4. No o - ver - plus, or need, no rich or poor were there,__ con - tent with dai - ly bread where

WORDS: Charles Wesley, MS Acts 71-2, in *Unpub. Poetry*, 2:295-96.
MUSIC: Carlton R. Young

all we cov-et here!_____ To him, and to each
could not dis-a-gree:_____ One soul did all the
he pos-sessed his own;_____ the dif-f'rent base of
all en-joyed their share;_____ with eve-ry com-mon

oth-er joined, they all were of one heart and
mem-bers move, the soul of har-mo-ny and
thine and *mine* was lost in char-i-ty Di-
bless-ing blessed, they noth-ing had, yet all pos-

1.2. 3.

mind.
love.
vine.

sessed.

Acts 4:32: The multitude of them that believed, were of one heart, and one soul; neither said any of them, that aught of the things which he possessed, was his own, but they had all things in common. Neither was there any among them that lacked.

1. Happy the multitude
        (but far above our sphere)
    redeemed by Jesus' blood
        from all we covet here!
    To him, and to each other joined,
    they all were of one heart and mind.

2. His blood the cement was
        who died on Calvary,
    and fastened to his cross
        they could not disagree:
    One soul did all the members move,
    the soul of harmony and love.

3. Their goods were free for all,
        appropriated to none,
    while none presumed to call
        what he possessed his own;
    the diff'rent base of *thine* and *mine*
    was lost in charity Divine.

4. No overplus, no need,
        no rich or poor were there,
    content with daily bread
        where all enjoyed their share;
    with every common blessing blessed
    they nothing had, yet all possessed.

16 You pastors hired who undertake

1. You pas-tors hired who un-der-take the awe-ful min-is-
2. See here an a-pos-tol-ic priest, com-mis-sioned from the
3. Je - sus, to us a-pos-tles raise, like-mind-ed pas-tors

try for lu-cre or am-bi-tion's sake, a nob-ler pat-tern
sky, who dares of all vain self di-vest, the need-y to sup-
give who free-ly may dis-pense your grace as free-ly they re-

see! Who greed-i - ly your pay re-ceive, and add-ing cure to
ply! A prim-i - tive ex-am-ple rare of gos-pel-pov-er-
ceive; who dis-en-gaged from all be-low may earth-ly things des-

cure, in splen - did ease and
ty, to feed the flock one's
pise, and eve - ry crea - ture -

WORDS: Charles Wesley, MS Acts, p. 75, in *Unpub. Poetry,* 2:298-99.
MUSIC: English melody (KINGSFOLD), arr. Ralph Vaughan Williams (1906)

plea - sures   live   by   pil - lag - ing   the   poor.
on - ly   care, and   like   the   Lord   to   be.
good fore - go   for   trea - sure   in   the   skies.

Acts 4:36-7: And Joses, who by the apostles was surnamed Barnabas (which is being interpreted, the son of consolation), a Levite, and of the country of Cyprus, having land, sold it and brought the money, and laid it at the apostles' feet.

1. You pastors hired who undertake
     the aweful ministry
  for lucre or ambition's sake,
     a nobler pattern see!
  Who greedily your pay receive,
     and adding cure to cure,
  in splendid ease and pleasure's live
     by pillaging the poor.

2. See here an apostolic priest,
     commissioned from the sky,
  who dare of all vain self divest,
     the needy to supply!
  A primitive example rare
     of gospel-poverty,
  to feed the flock one's only care,
     and like the Lord to be.

3. Jesus, to us apostle's raise,
     like-minded pastors give
  who freely may dispense your grace
     as freely they receive;
  who disengaged from all below
     may earthly things despise,
  and every creature-good forego
     for treasure in the skies.

143

Bibliography

Allchin, A. M. *Participation in God: A Forgotten Strand in Anglican Theology*. Wilton, CT: Morehouse-Barlow, 1988.

Bailey, William. *A Treatise on the Better Employment, and more Comfortable Support, of the Poor in Workhouses; together with some observations on the growth and culture of flax: with divers new inventions, neatly engraved on copper, for the improvement of linen manufacture, of which the importance and advantages are considered and evinced*. London: Dodsley, 1758.

Baker, Frank, editor. *Representative Verse of Charles Wesley*. New York: Abingdon, 1962.

Beattie, J. M. *Crime and Courts in England, 1660–1800*. Princeton: Princeton University Press, 1986.

Bouteneff, Peter. "All Creation in United Thanksgiving: Gregory of Nyssa and the Wesleys on Salvation." In *Orthodox and Wesleyan Spirituality*, edited by S T Kimbrough Jr., 189–204. Crestwood, NY: St. Vladimir's Seminary Press, 2002.

Campbell, Ted A. "Charles Wesley *Theologos*." In *Charles Wesley: Life, Literature and Legacy*, edited by Kenneth G. C. Newport and Ted A. Campbell, 264–77. Peterborough: Epworth, 2007.

Chilcote, Paul W., editor. *The Wesleyan Tradition: A Paradigm for Renewal*. Nashville: Abingdon, 2002.

Christiansen, Michael J., and Jeffrey Wittung, editors. *Partakers of the Life Divine*. Madison, NJ: Fairleigh Dickinson University Press, 2006.

Dayton, Donald. "The Wesleyan Option for the Poor." *Wesleyan Theological Journal* 26:1 (1991) 7–22.

Hay, Douglas, et al. *Albion's Fatal Tree: Crime and Society in Eighteenth-Century England*. London: Allen Lane, 1975.

Heitzenrater, Richard P., editor. *The Poor and the People Called Methodists, 1729–1999*. Nashville: Kingswood, 2002.

———. *Wesley and the People Called Methodists*. Nashville: Abingdon, 1995.

Hildebrandt, Franz, and Oliver A. Beckerlegge, editors. *A Collection of Hymns for the Use of the People Called Methodists*. Nashville: Abingdon, 1983. *The Bicentennial Edition of the Works of John Wesley*, vol. 7.

Holbert, John, S T Kimbrough Jr., and Carlton R. Young, editors. *Psalms for Praise and Worship*. Nashville: Abingdon, 1992.

Holroyd, John Baker, Earl of Sheffield. *Observations on the Impolicy, Abuses, and False Interpretations of the Poor Laws; and on the Reports of the Two Houses of Parliament*. 2nd edition. London: Printed for J. Hatchard, 1818.

Hughes, Robert. "Wesleyan Roots of Christian Socialism." *The Ecumenist* 13 (1975) 49–53.

Jennings, Theodore W., Jr. *Good News to the Poor: John Wesley's Evangelical Economics*. Nashville: Abingdon, 1990.

Kimbrough, S T, Jr. "Charles Wesley and the Poor." In *The Portion of the Poor: Good News to the Poor in the Wesleyan Tradition*, edited by M. Douglas Meeks, 147–67. Nashville: Kingswood, 1995.

———. *The Lyrical Theology of Charles Wesley: A Reader*. Eugene, OR: Cascade, 2010.

———, editor. *Orthodox and Wesleyan Ecclesiology*. Crestwood, NY: St. Vladimir's Seminary Press, 2007.

———. *Orthodox and Wesleyan Spirituality*. Crestwood, NY: St. Vladimir's Seminary Press, 2002.

———. "Perfection Revisited: Charles Wesley's Theology of 'Gospel Poverty' and 'Perfect Poverty.'" In *The Poor and the People Called Methodists, 1729–1999*, edited by Richard P. Heitzenrater, 101–19. Nashville: Kingswood, 2002.

———. "Theosis in the Writings of Charles Wesley." *St. Vladimir's Theological Seminary Quarterly* 52:2 (2008) 199–212.

Kimbrough, S T, Jr., and Carlton R. Young, editors. *Help Us to Help Each Other: Songs for Life and Ministry with the Poor by Charles Wesley*. Madison, NJ: Charles Wesley Society, 2010.

———. *John Wesley's First Tune Book: A Collection of Tunes Set to Music, As They Are Commonly Sung at the Foundery*. London: A Pearson, 1742. A Facsimile Edition with Introduction and Notes. Madison, NJ: Charles Wesley Society, 2010.

Kimbrough, S T, Jr., Timothy E. Kimbrough, and Carlton R. Young, editors. *Songs for the Poor: Singer's Edition*. New York: General Board of Global Ministries, 1997.

King, Peter. *Crime, Justice, and Discretion in England, 1740–1820*. New York: Oxford University Press, 2000.

Maddox, Randy L. *Responsible Grace: John Wesley's Practical Theology*. Nashville: Kingswood, 1994.

Marquardt, Manfred. *Praxis und Prinzipien der Sozialethik John Wesleys*. Göttingen: Vandenhoeck & Ruprecht, 1977. English translation by John E. Steely and W. Stephen Gunter. Nashville: Abingdon, 1992.

Meeks, M. Douglas. *God the Economist: The Doctrine of God and Political Economy*. Minneapolis: Fortress, 1989.

———, editor. *The Portion of the Poor: Good News to the Poor in the Wesleyan Tradition*. Nashville: Kingswood, 1995.

M'Farlan, John. *Inquiries Concerning the Poor*. Edinburgh: Dickins, 1782.

Miles, Rebekah, "Works of Mercy as Spiritual Formation." In *Wesleyan Tradition: A Paradigm for Renewal*, 98–110, edited by Paul W. Chilcote. Nashville: Abingdon, 2002.

Newport, Kenneth G. C., editor. *The Sermons of Charles Wesley: A Critical Edition, with Introduction and Notes*. Oxford: Oxford University Press, 2001.

Newport, Kenneth G. C., and Ted A. Campbell, editors. *Charles Wesley: Life, Literature and Legacy*. Peterborough: Epworth, 2007.

Rattenbury, J. Ernest. *Evangelical Doctrines of Charles Wesley's Hymns*. London: Epworth, 1941.

Rieger, Joerg. *Remember the Poor: The Challenge of Theology in the Twenty-First Century*. Harrisburg, PA: Trinity, 1998.

Runyon, Theodore, editor. *Sanctification and Liberation: Liberation Theologies in Light of the Wesleyan Tradition*. Nashville: Abingdon, 1981.

Tamez, Elsa. "Wesley as Read by the Poor." In *The Future of Methodist Theological Traditions*, edited by M. Douglas Meeks, 67–84. Nashville: Abingdon, 1985.

Tindley, Charles Albert. *Beams of Heaven: Hymns of Charles Albert Tindley*, edited by S T Kimbrough Jr. and Carlton R. Young. New York: General Board of Global Ministries, 2006.

Townsend, Joseph. *Dissertation on the Poor Laws, by a Well-wisher to Mankind*. London: C. Dilly, 1786.

Tyson, John. *Charles Wesley on Sanctification: A Biographical and Theological Study*. Salem, OH: Schmul, 1992.

Vassiliadis, Petros. *Eucharist and Witness*. Geneva: WCC, 1998.

Walsh, John. "John Wesley and the Community of Goods." In *Protestant Evangelicalism: Britain, Ireland, Germany, and America, c. 1750–c. 1950: Essays in Honor of W. Reginald Ward*, edited by Keith Robbins, 25–50. Oxford: Blackwell, 1990.

Warner, Wellman Joel. *The Wesleyan Movement in the Industrial Revolution*. New York: Russell & Russell, 1967.

White, Susan. "Charles Wesley and Contemporary Theology." In *Charles Wesley: Life, Literature and Legacy*, edited by Kenneth G. C. Newport and Ted A. Campbell, 515–31. Peterborough: Epworth, 2007.

Wiseman, Luke. *Charles Wesley, Evangelist and Poet*. New York: Abingdon, 1931.

Woloch, Isser. *Eighteenth-Century Europe: Tradition and Progress, 1715–1789*. New York: Norton, 1982.

Young, Carlton R. *Music of the Heart*. Carol Stream, IL: Hope, 1995.

———, editor. *The United Methodist Hymnal*. Nashville: United Methodist Publishing House, 1989.

Young, Frances. "Inner Struggle: Some Parallels between the Spirituality of John Wesley and the Greek Fathers." In *Orthodox and Wesleyan Spirituality*, edited by S T Kimbrough Jr., 157–72. Crestwood, NY: St. Vladimir's Seminary Press, 2002.

WORKS OF JOHN AND CHARLES WESLEY

Osborn, George, editor. *Poetical Works of John and Charles Wesley*. 13 vols. London: Wesleyan Methodist Conference, 1868–72.

[Wesley, John and Charles]. *Hymns for Times of Trouble and Persecution*. [London: Strahan, 1744].

Wesley, John and Charles. *Collection of Psalms and Hymns*. 2nd ed., enlarged. London: Strahan, 1743.

———. *Hymns and Sacred Poems*. London: Strahan, 1739.

———. *Hymns and Sacred Poems*. London: Strahan, 1740.

———. *Hymns and Sacred Poems*. Bristol: Farley, 1742.

———. *Hymns of Petition and Thanksgiving for the Promise of the Father: Hymns for Whitsunday*. Bristol: Farley, 1746.

WORKS OF CHARLES WESLEY

Baker, Frank, editor. *Representative Verse of Charles Wesley*. London: Epworth, 1962.

Kimbrough, S T, Jr., and Oliver A. Beckerlegge, editors. *The Unpublished Poetry of Charles Wesley*. 3 vols. Nashville: Kingswood, 1988–1992.

[Wesley, Charles]. *Funeral Hymns*. London: [Strahan,] 1759.

———. *Hymns of Intercession for All Mankind*. Bristol: Farley, 1758.

Wesley, Charles. *Elegy on the Death of Robert Jones, Esq. of Fonmon Castle in Glamorganshire, South Wales.* Bristol: Farley, 1742.

———. *Hymns and Sacred Poems,* 2 vols. Bristol: Farley, 1749.

———. *Hymns for Those That Seek and Those That Have Redemption in the Blood of Jesus Christ.* London: Strahan, 1747.

———. *The Manuscript Journal of the Reverend Charles Wesley, M.A.,* 2 vols. Edited by S T Kimbrough, Jr. and Kenneth G. C. Newport. Nashville: Abingdon, 2007.

———. *Short Hymns on Select Passages of the Holy Scriptures.* 2 vols. Bristol: Farley, 1762.

Index of Scripture References

Index of Personal Names

Subject Index